Shape & Shadow
Grayscale Adult Coloring

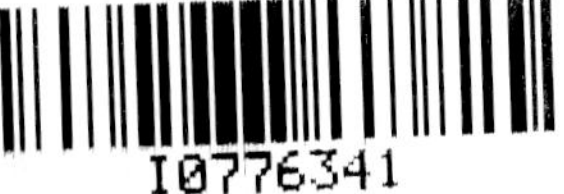

Cate Edwards

ISBN-13:978-1979392396

ISBN-10:1979392390

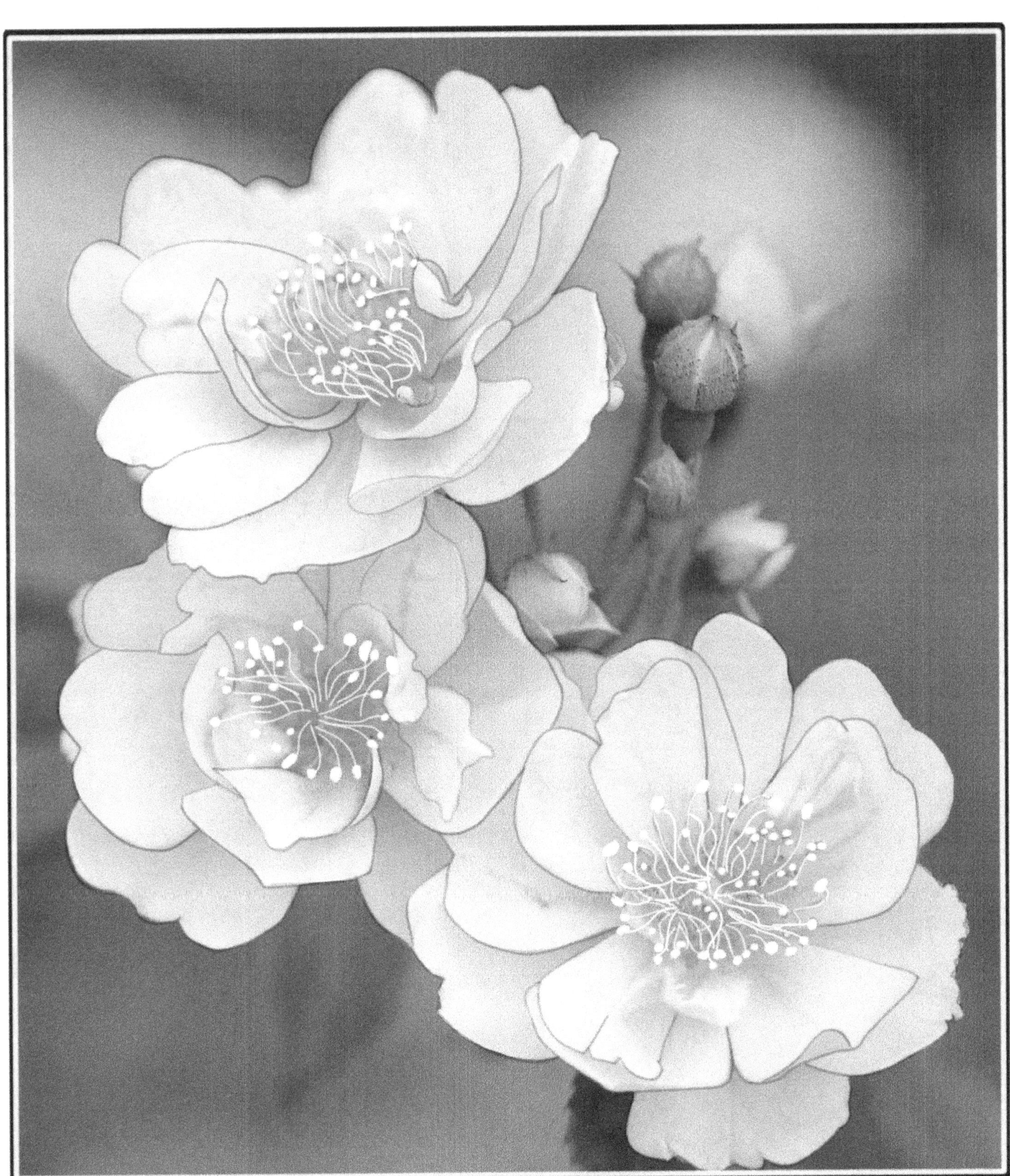

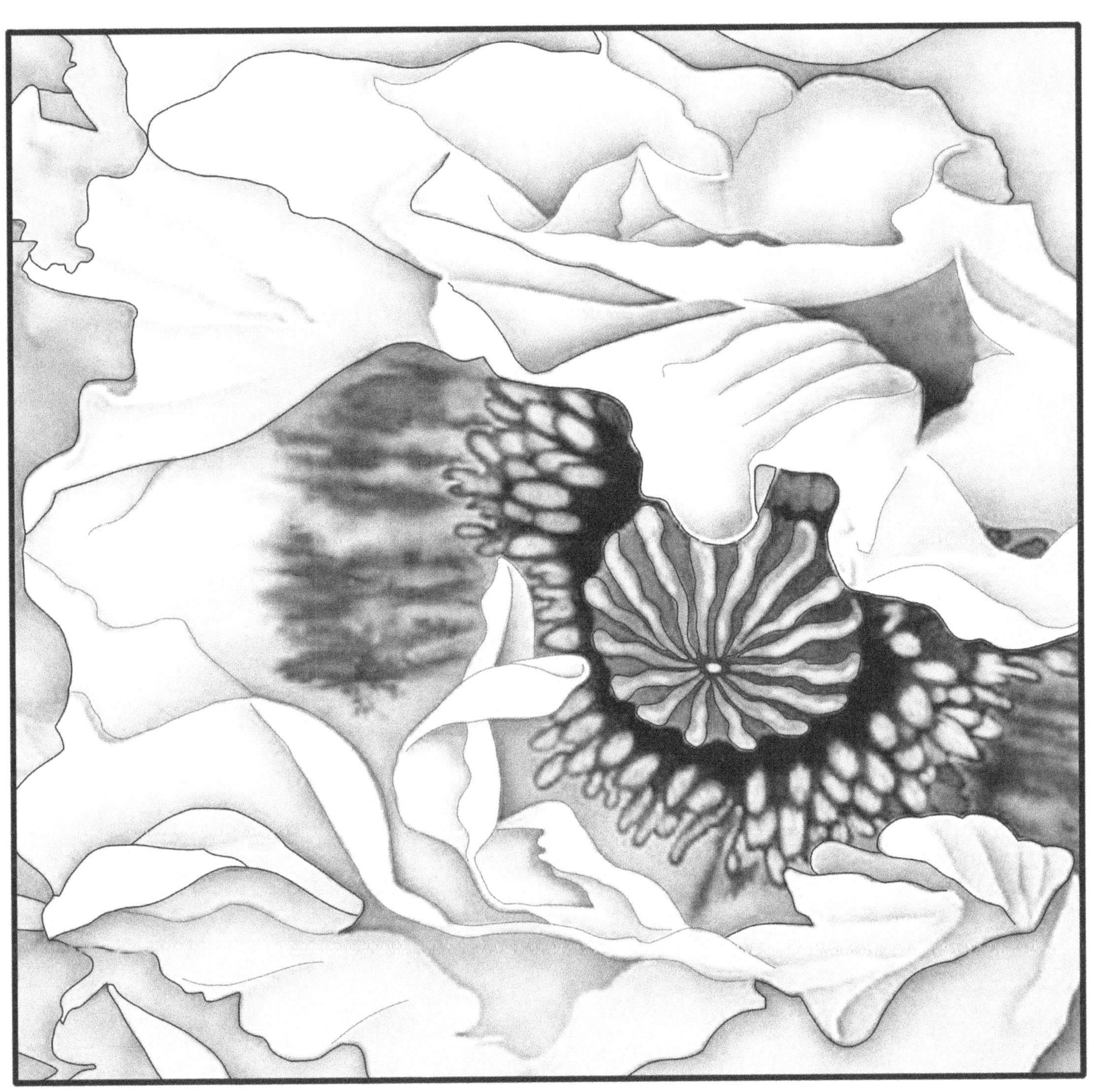

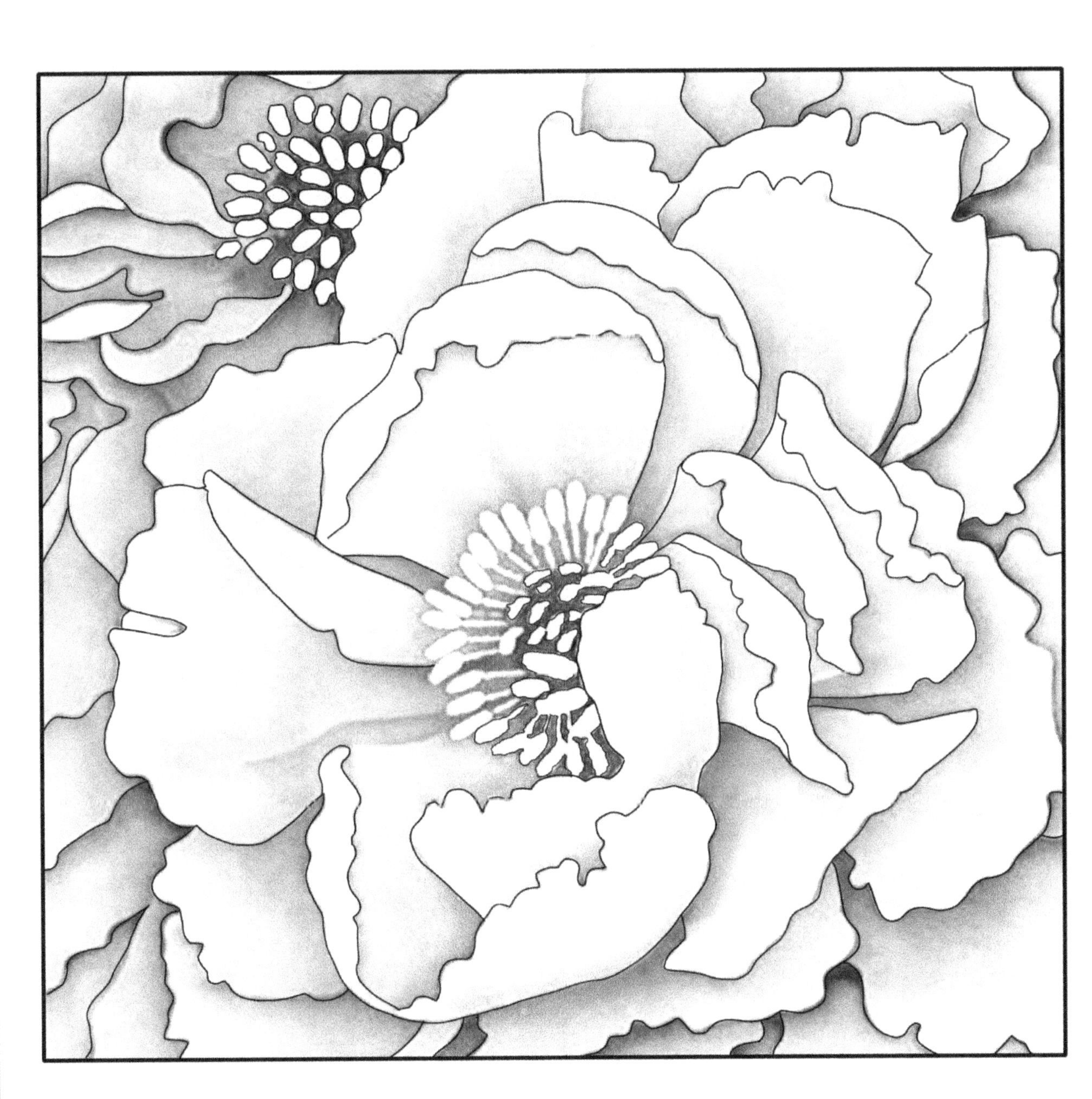

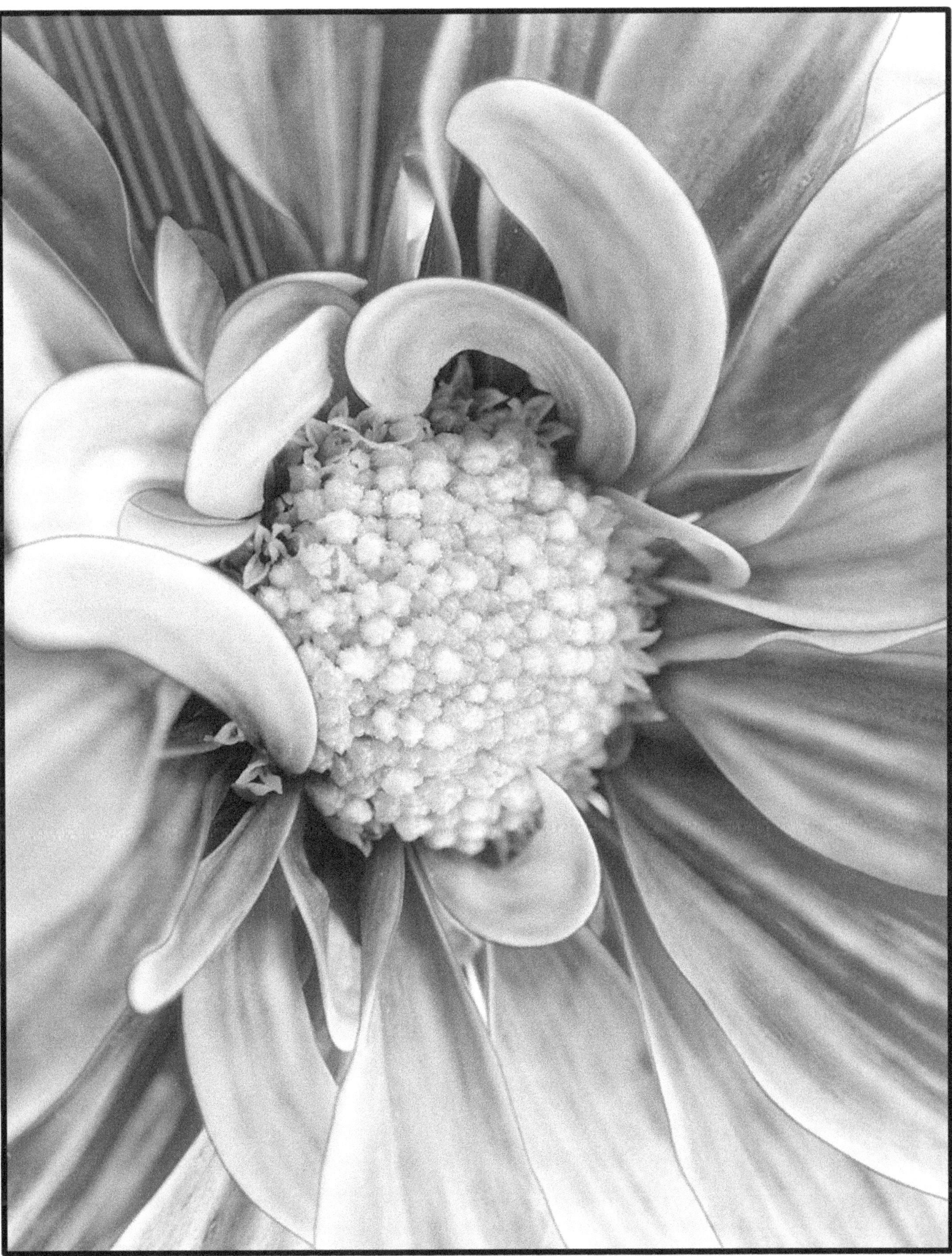

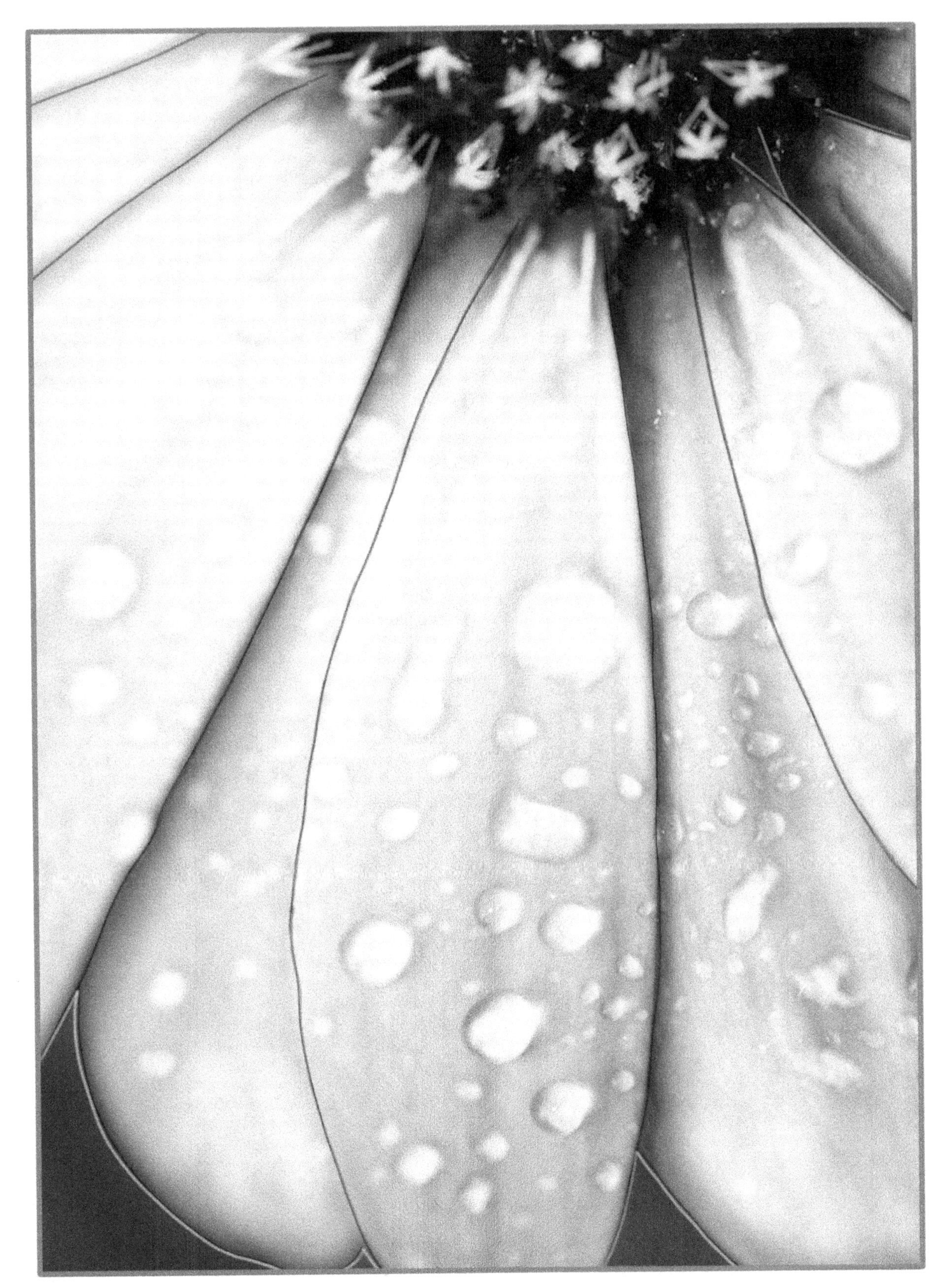

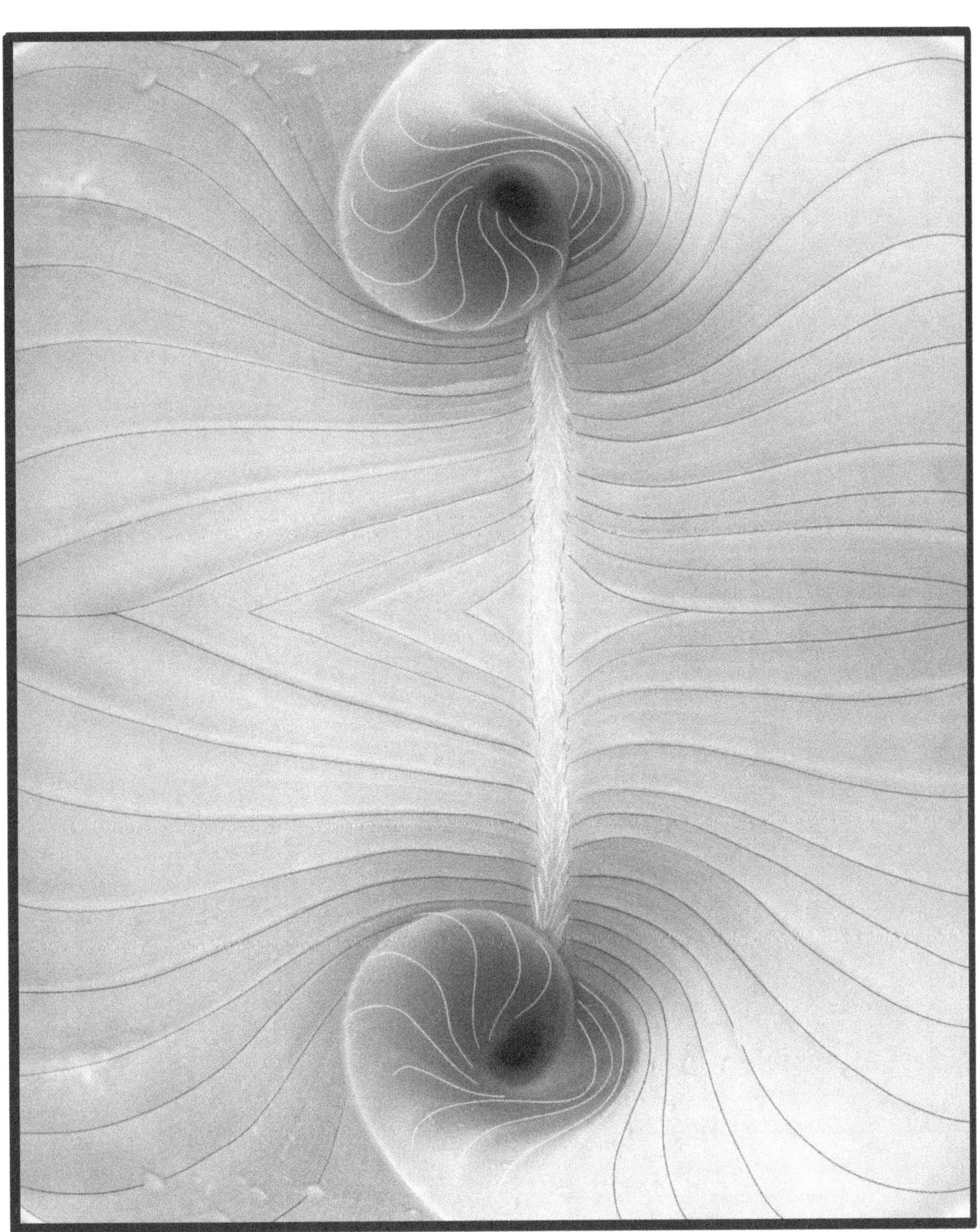

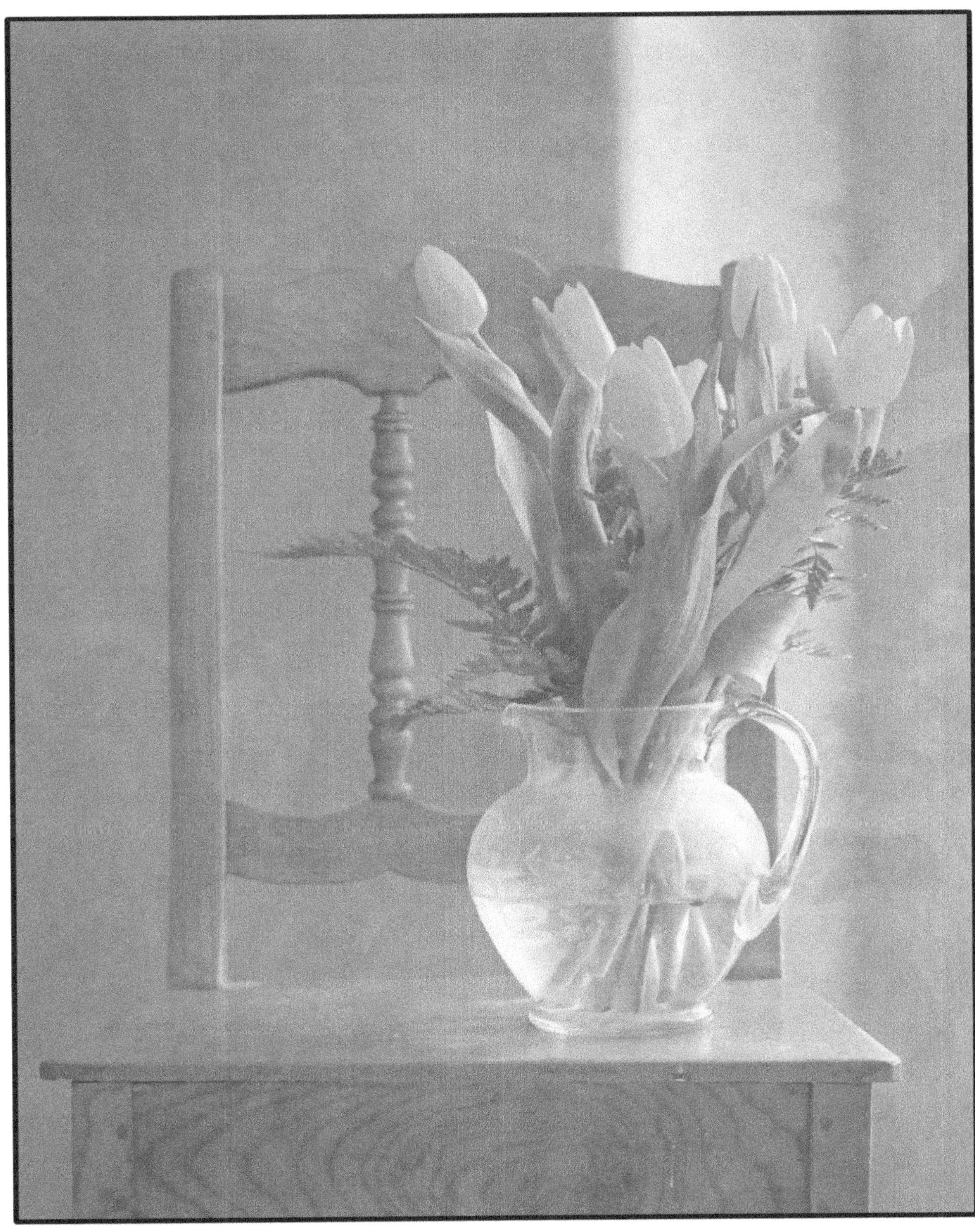

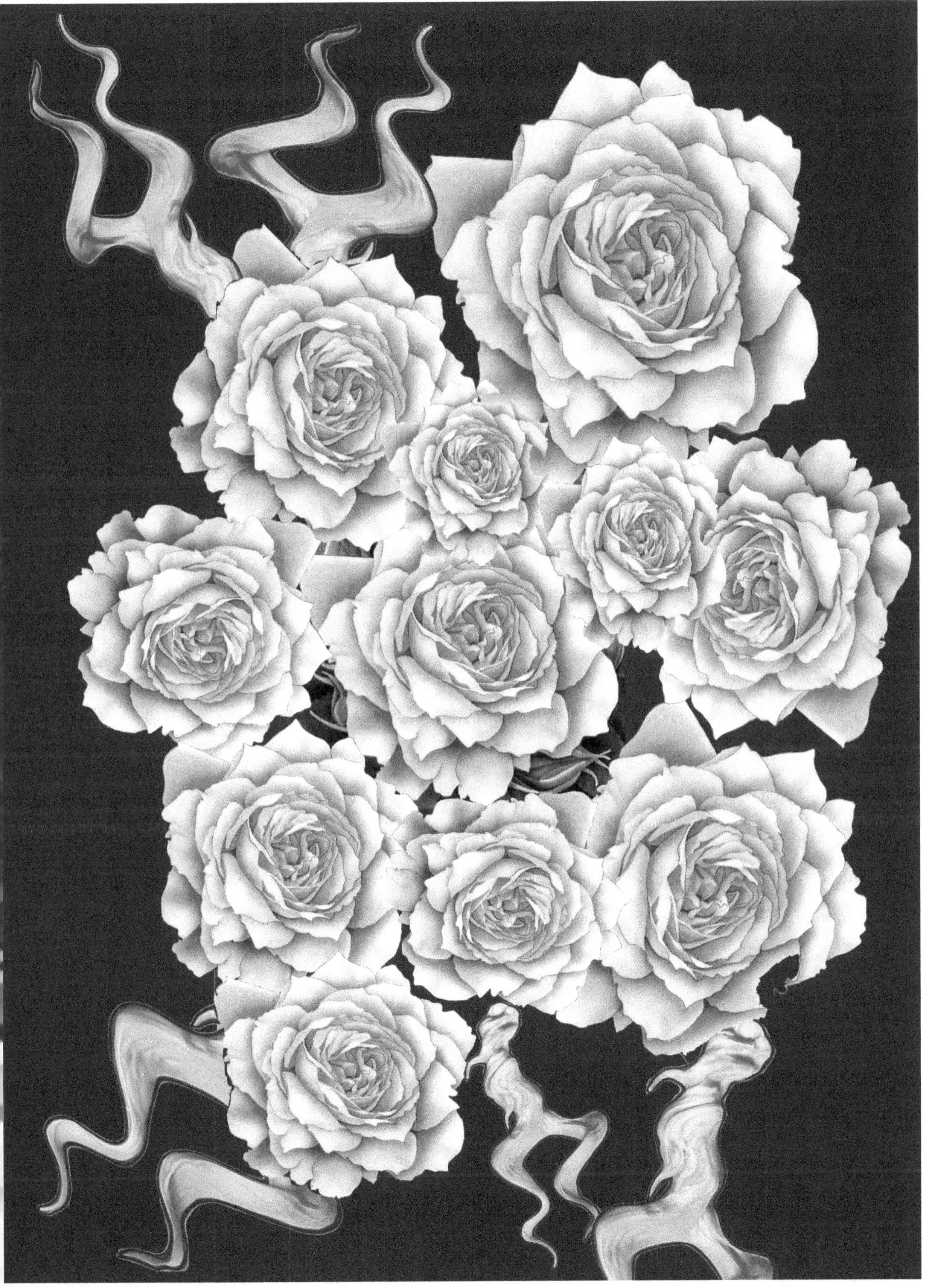

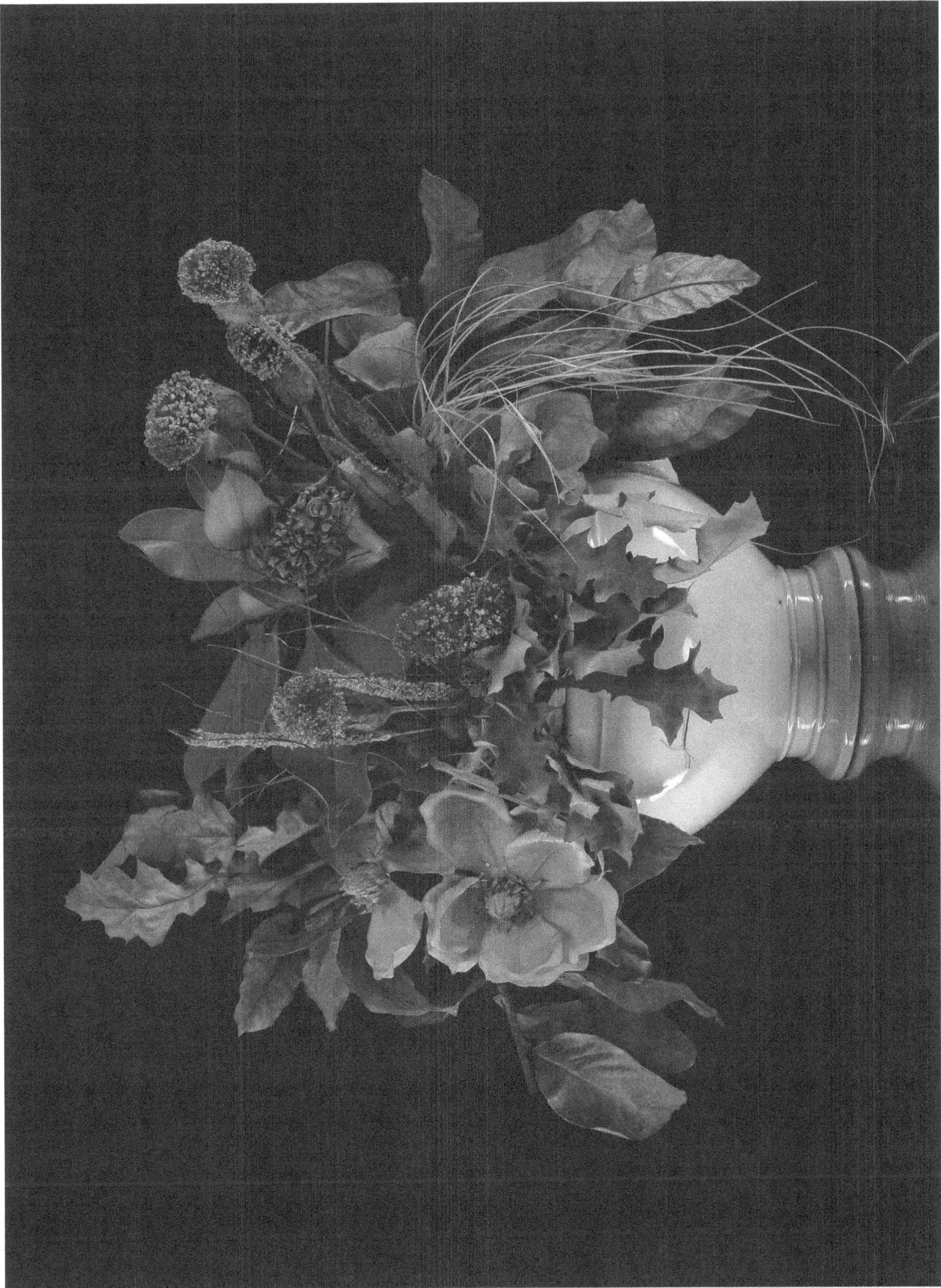

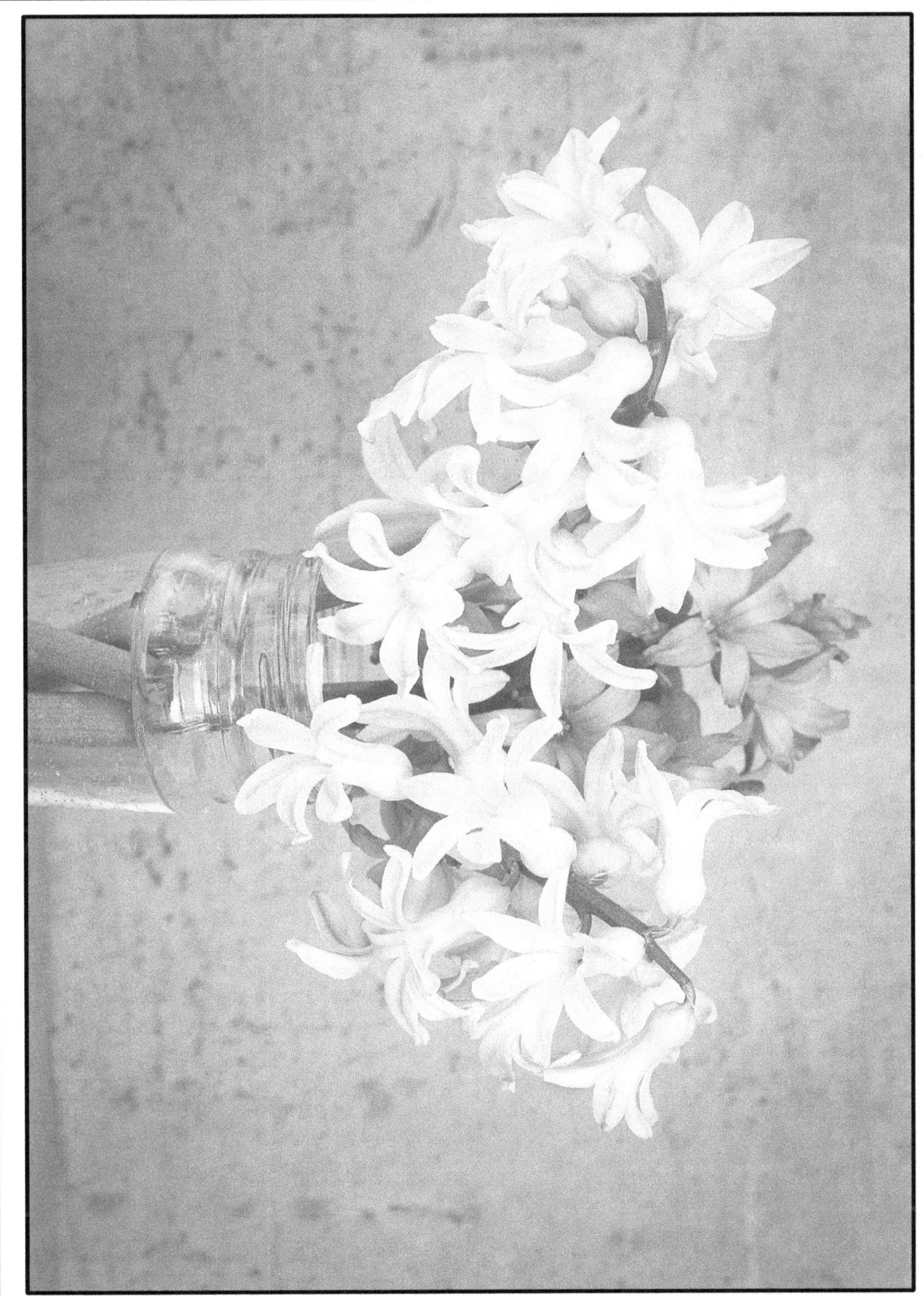

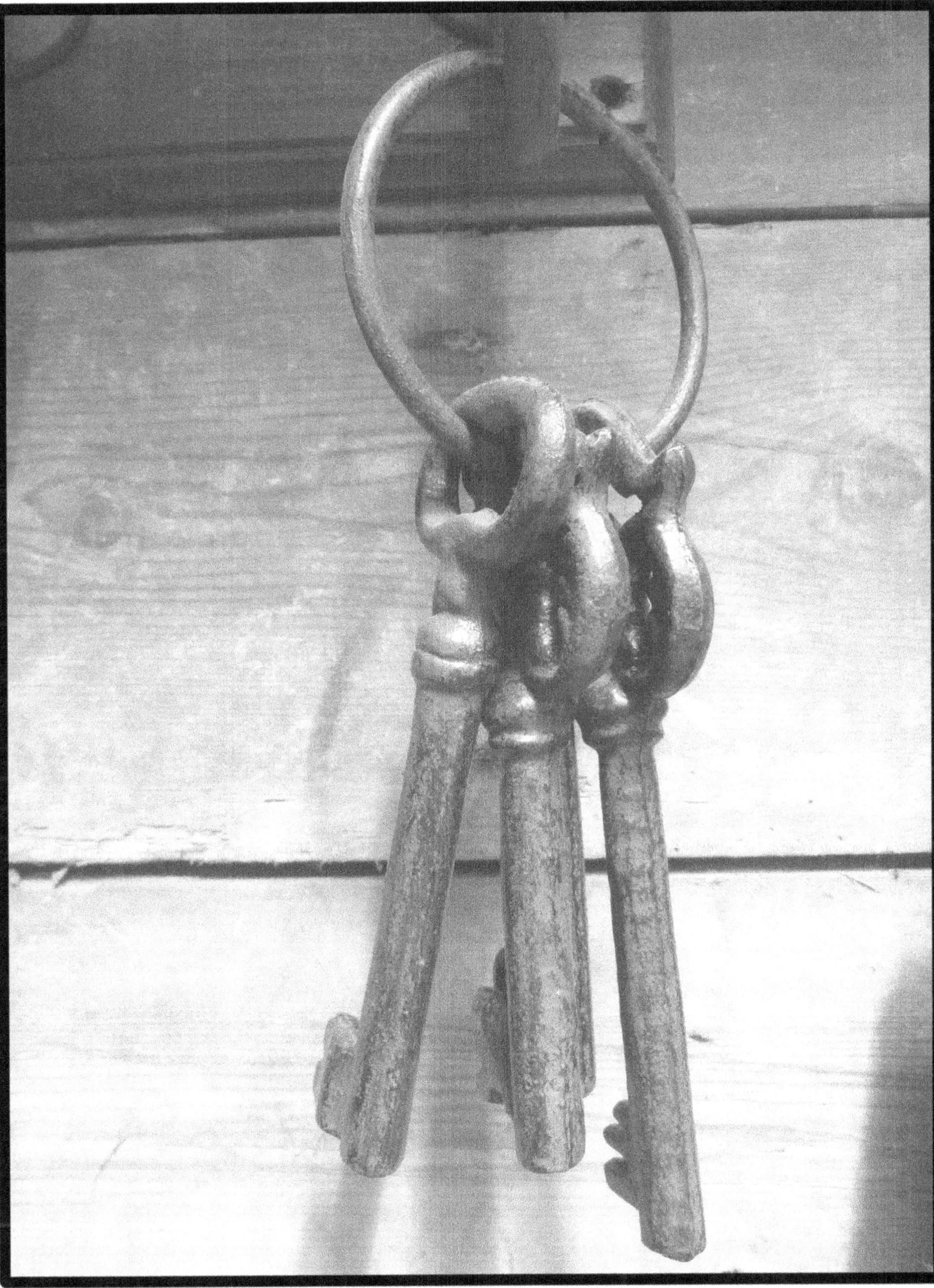

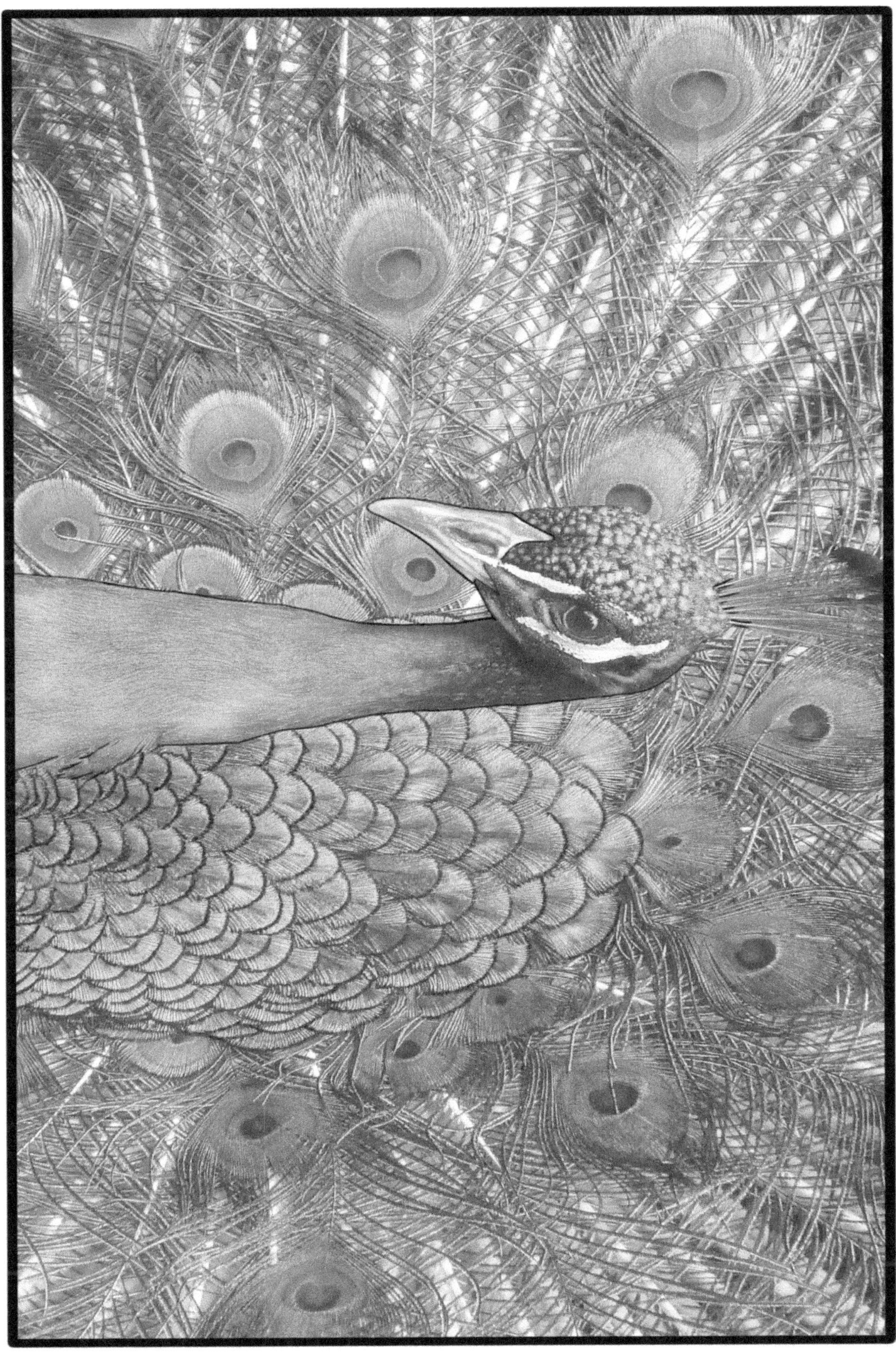

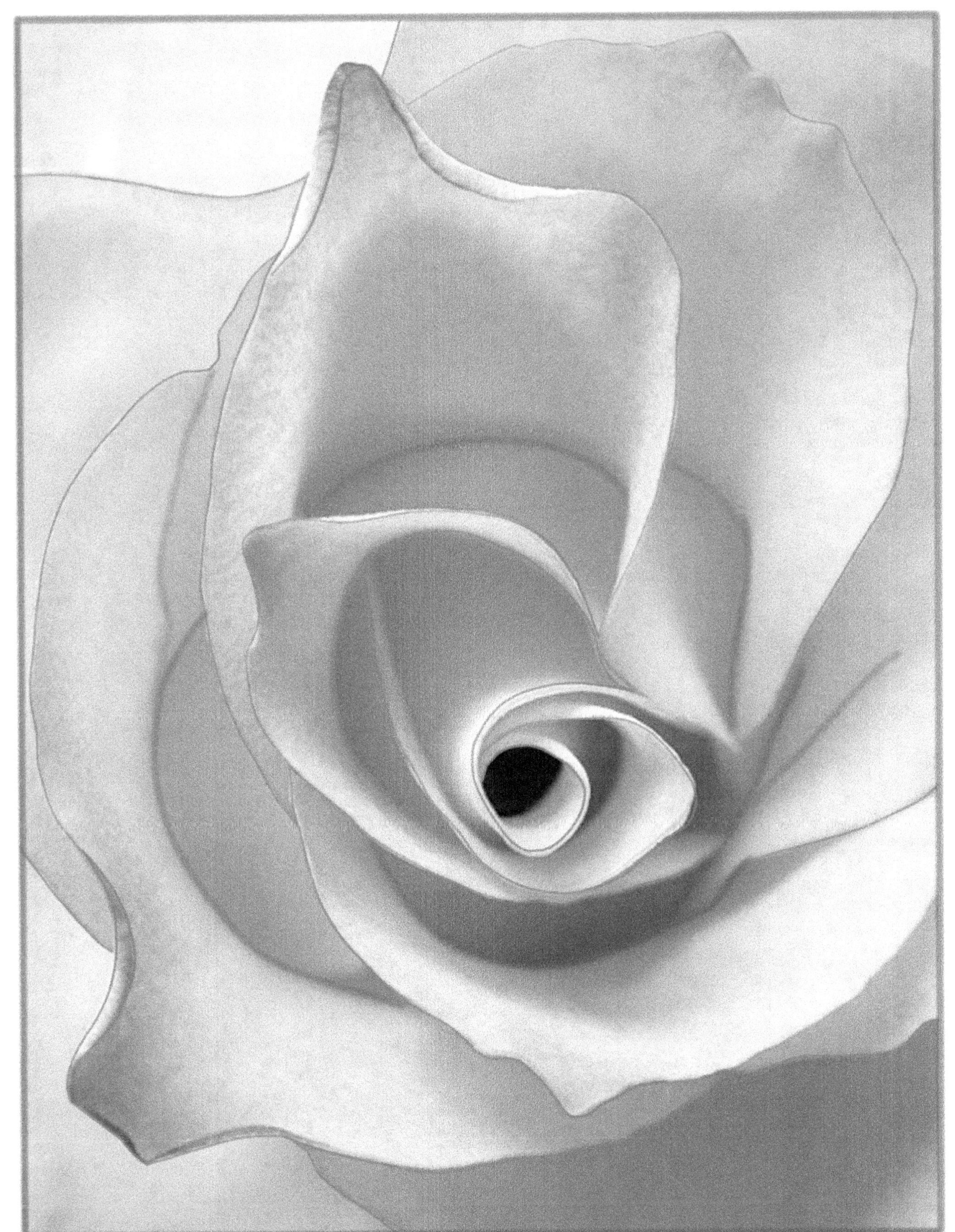

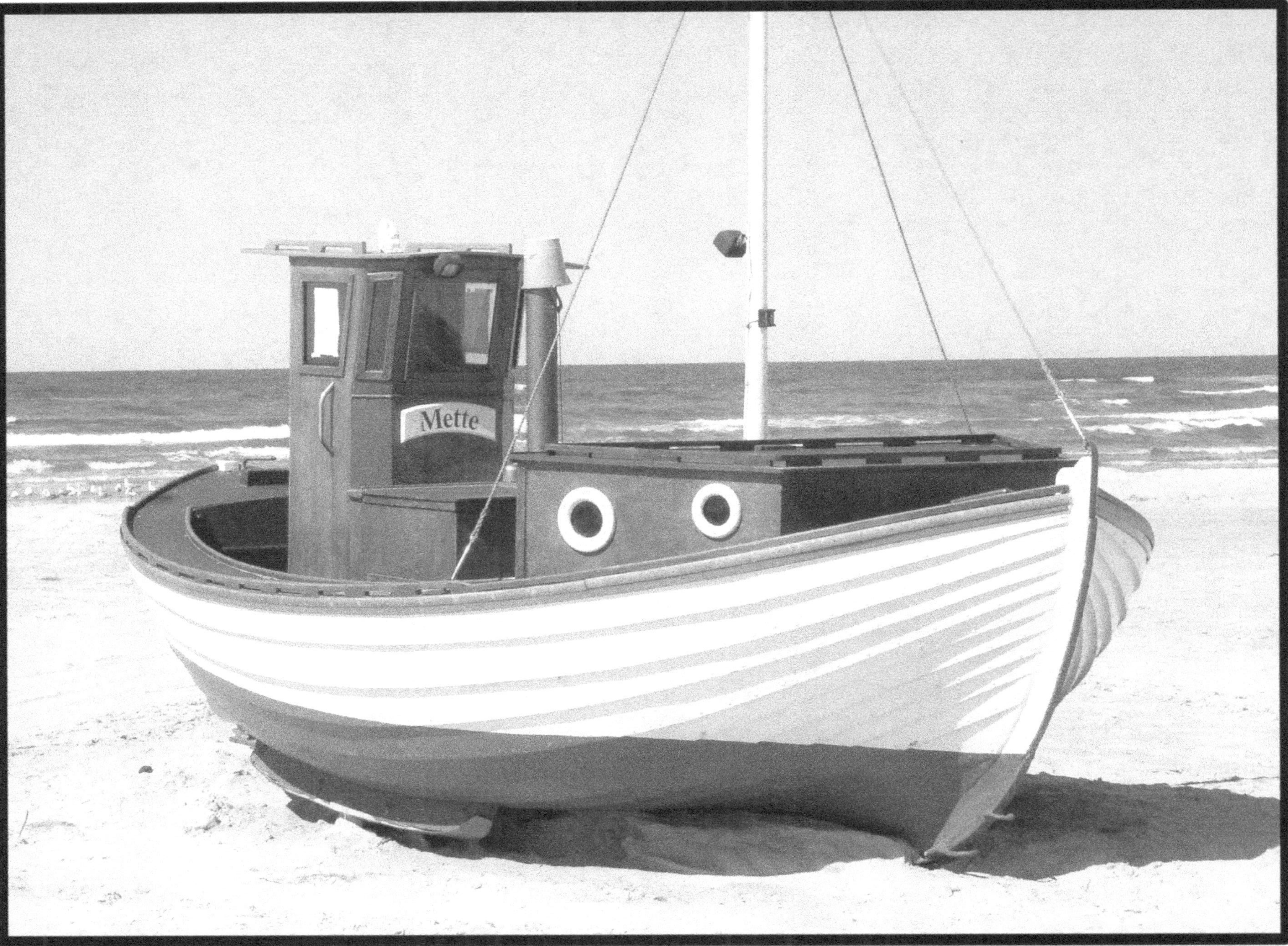
Mette

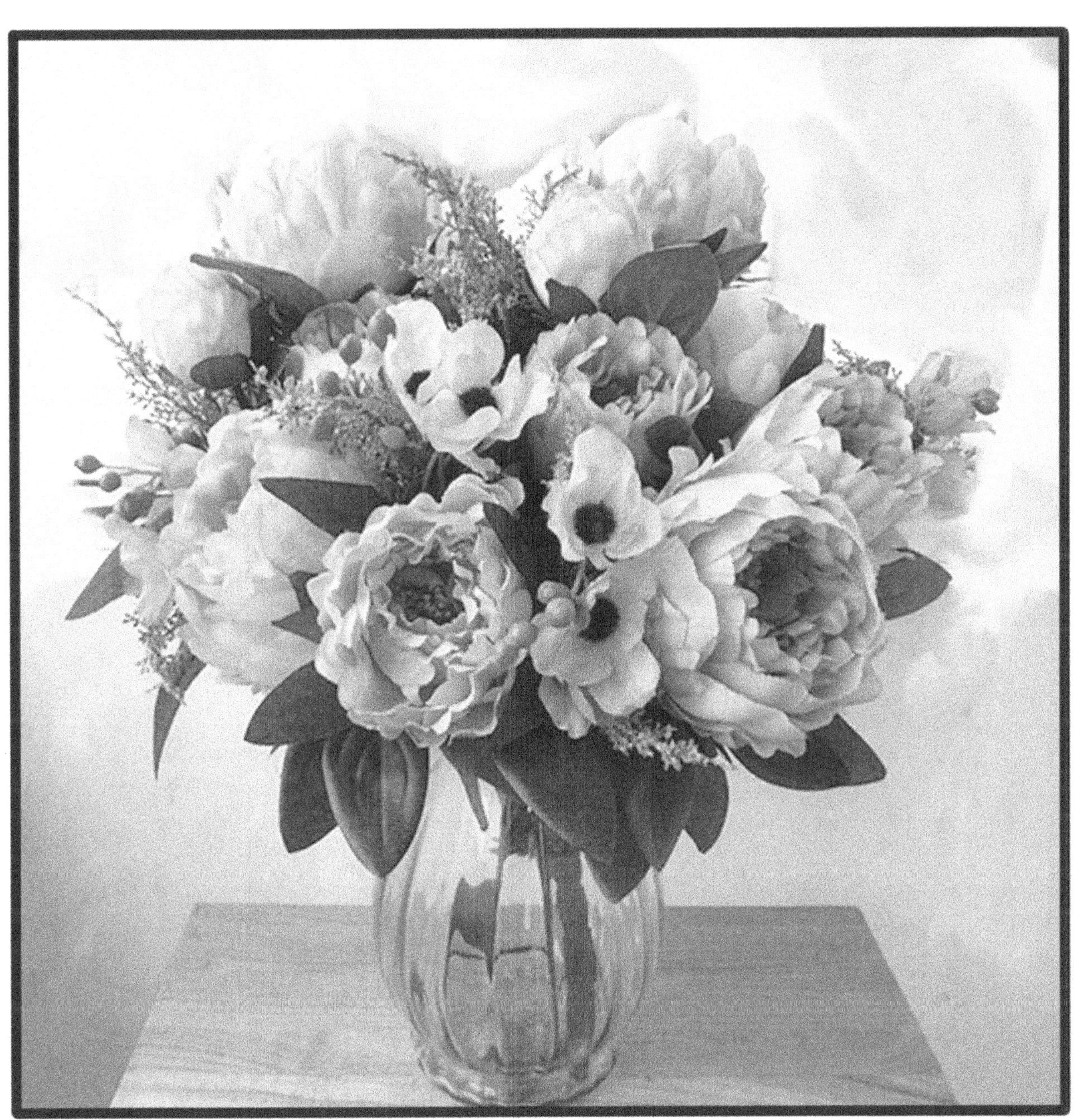

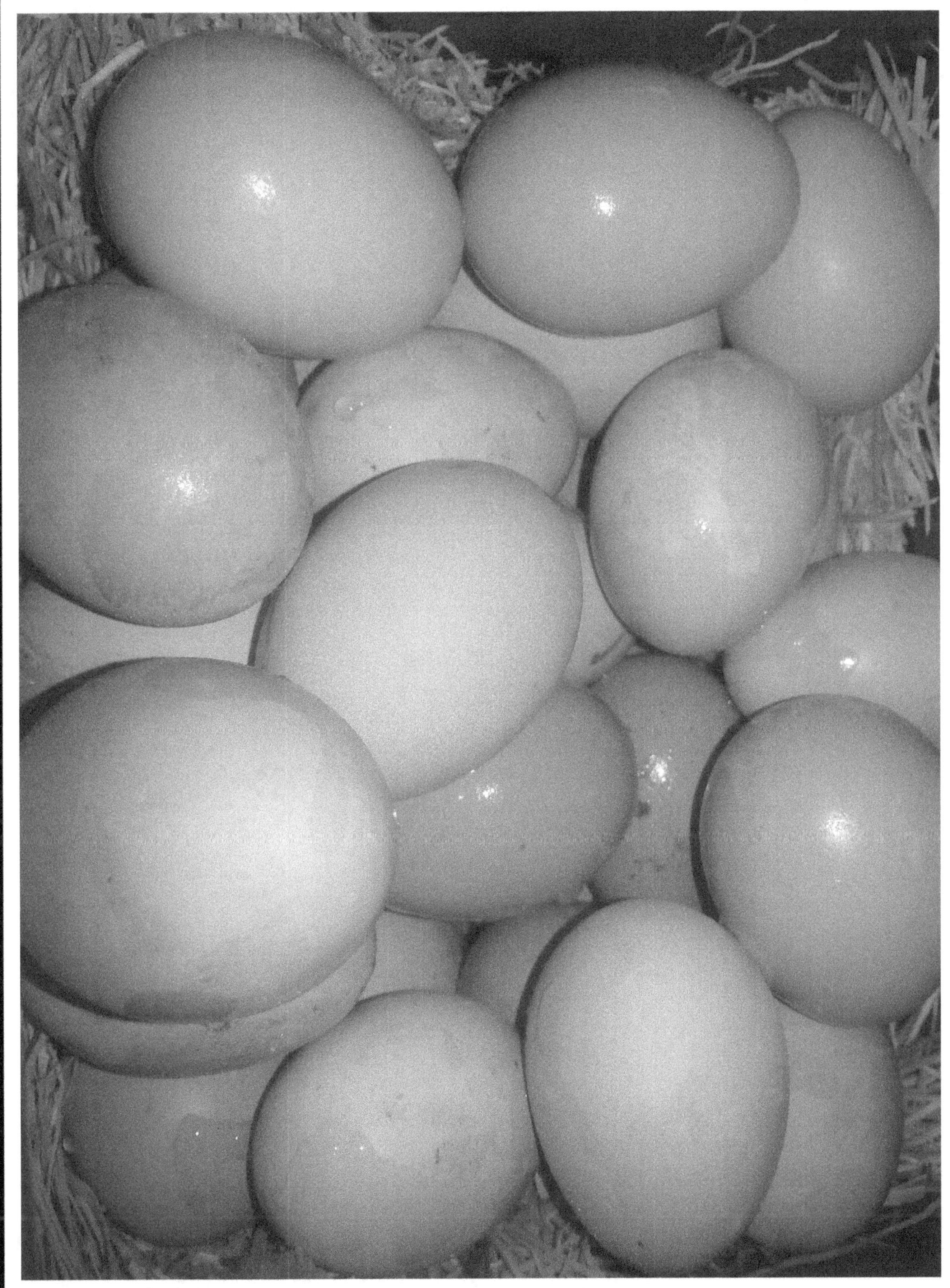

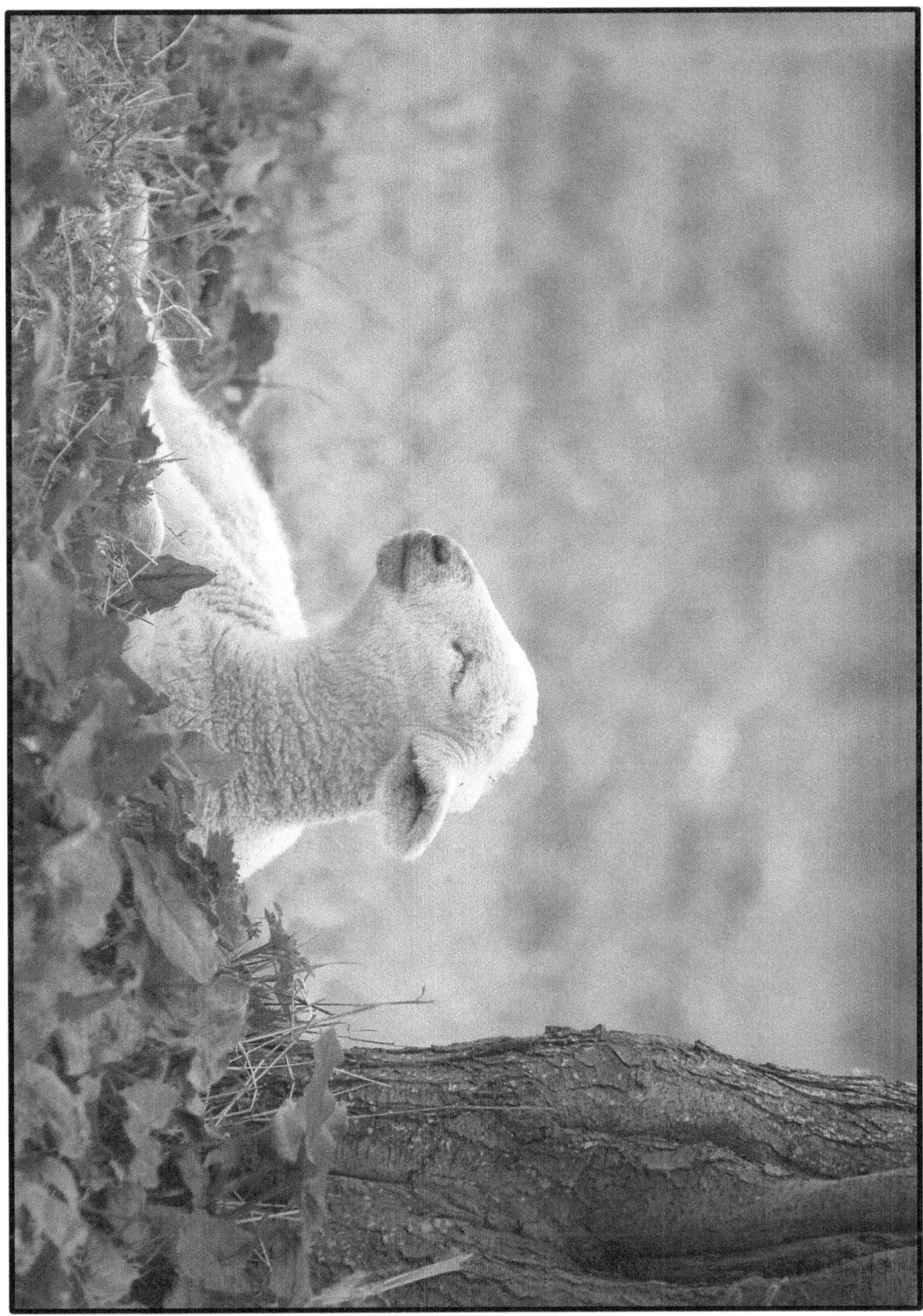

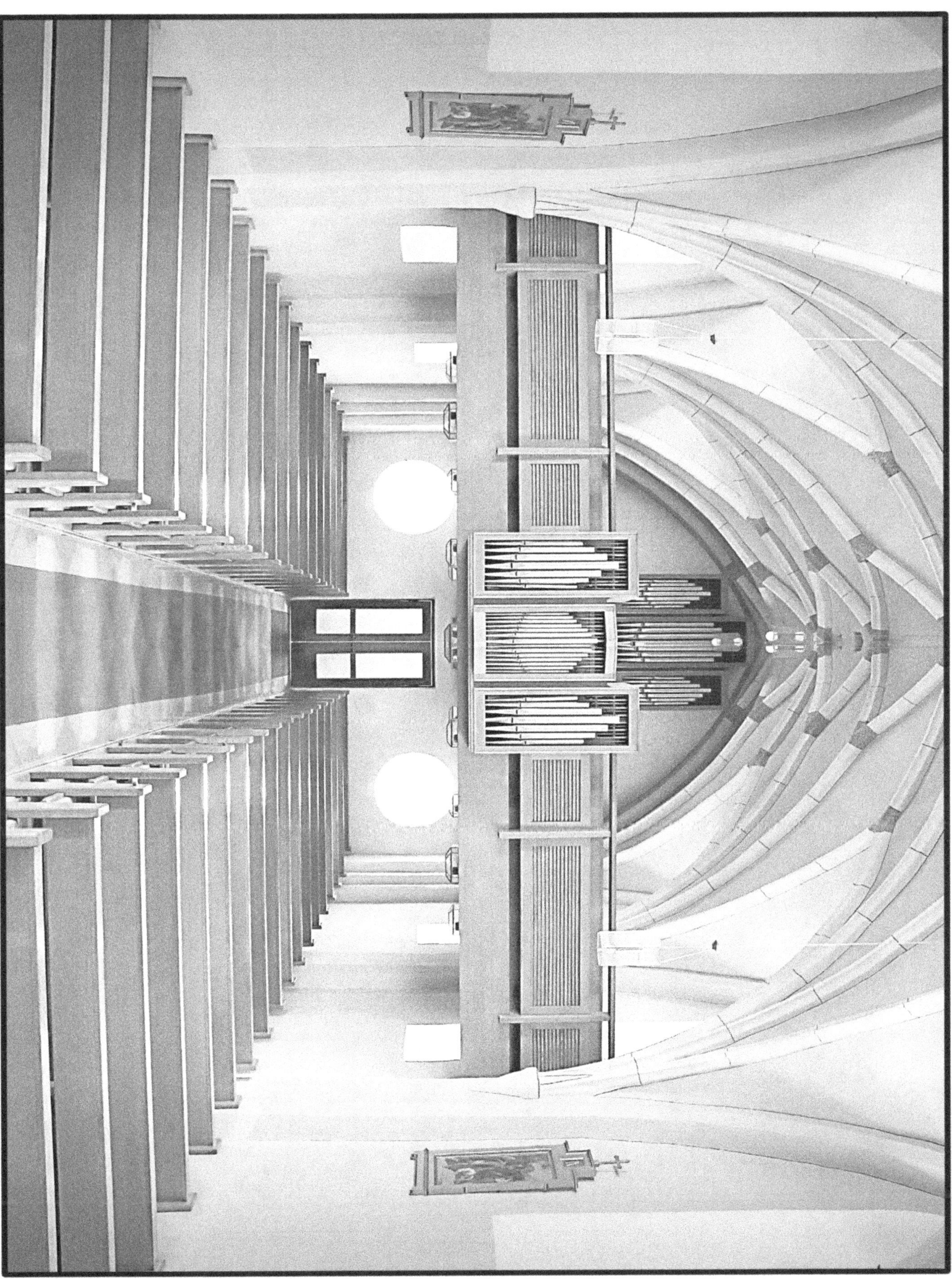

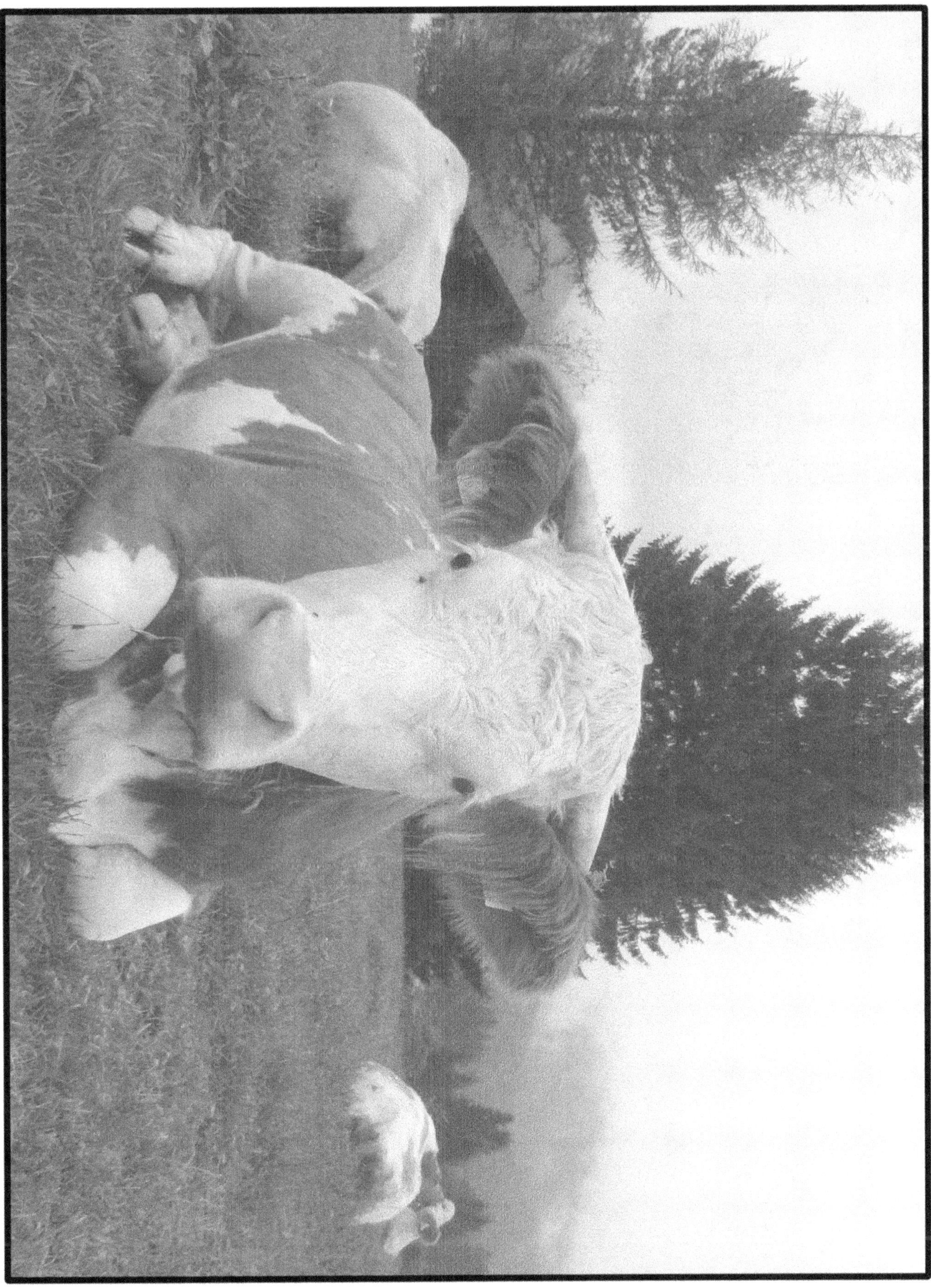

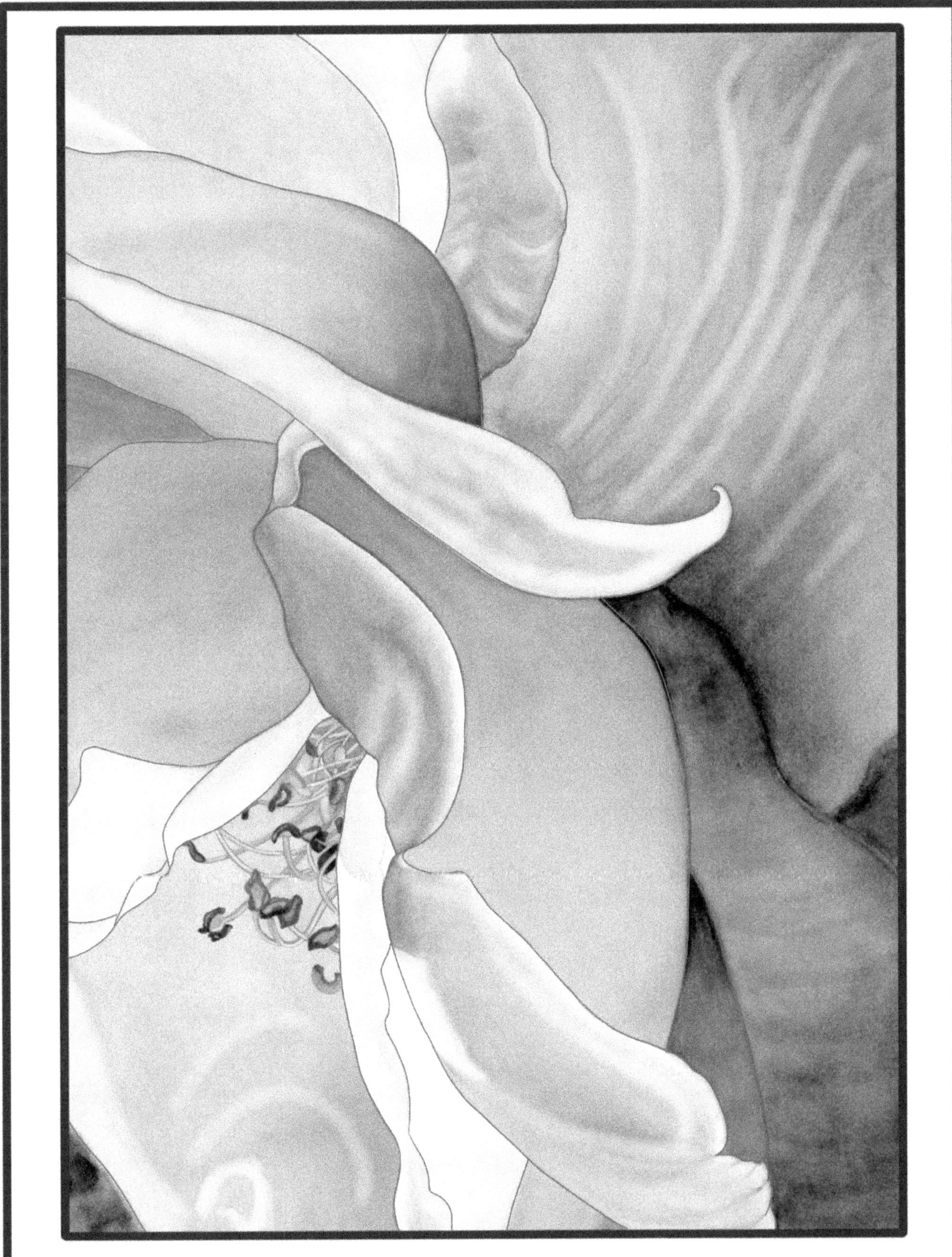

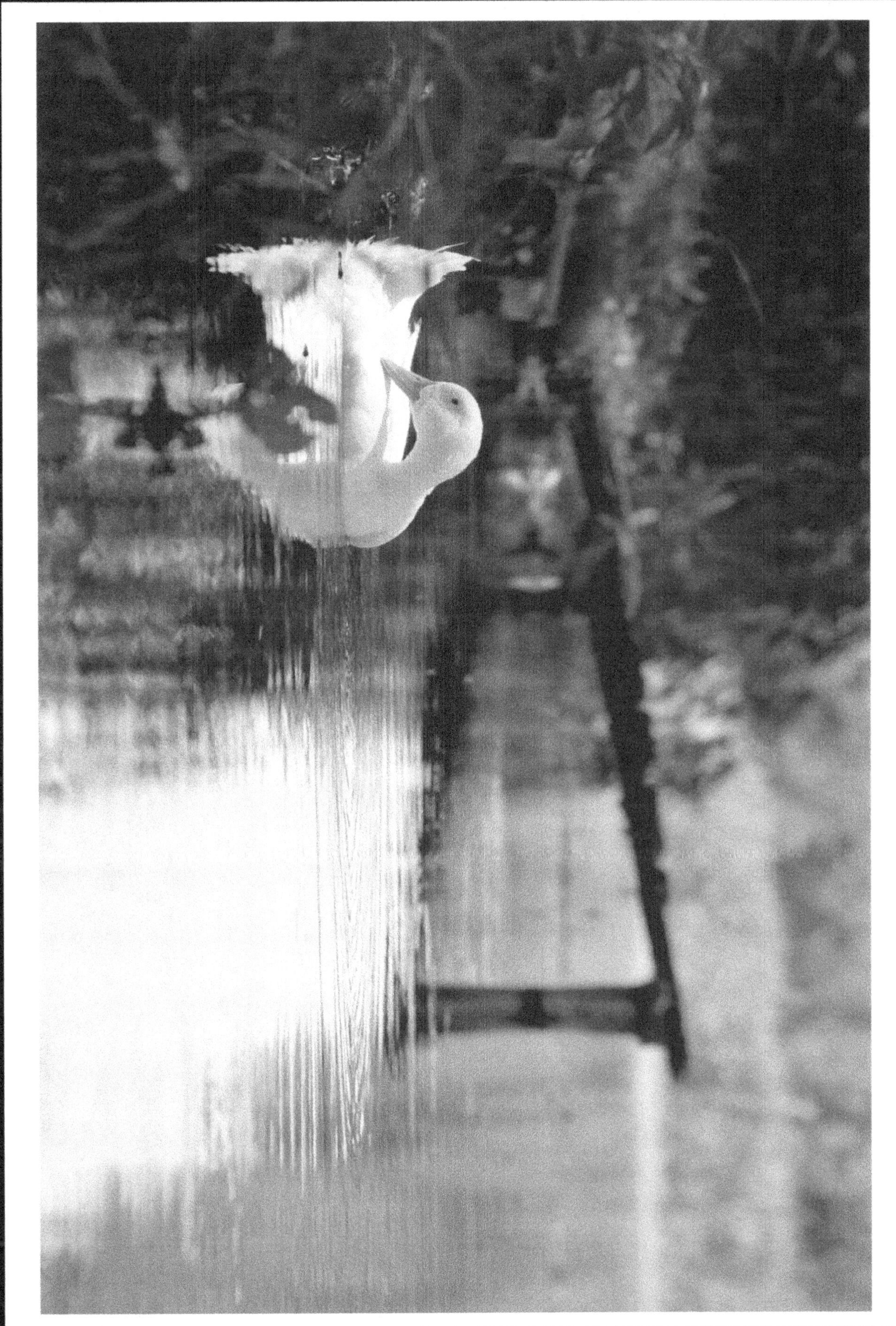

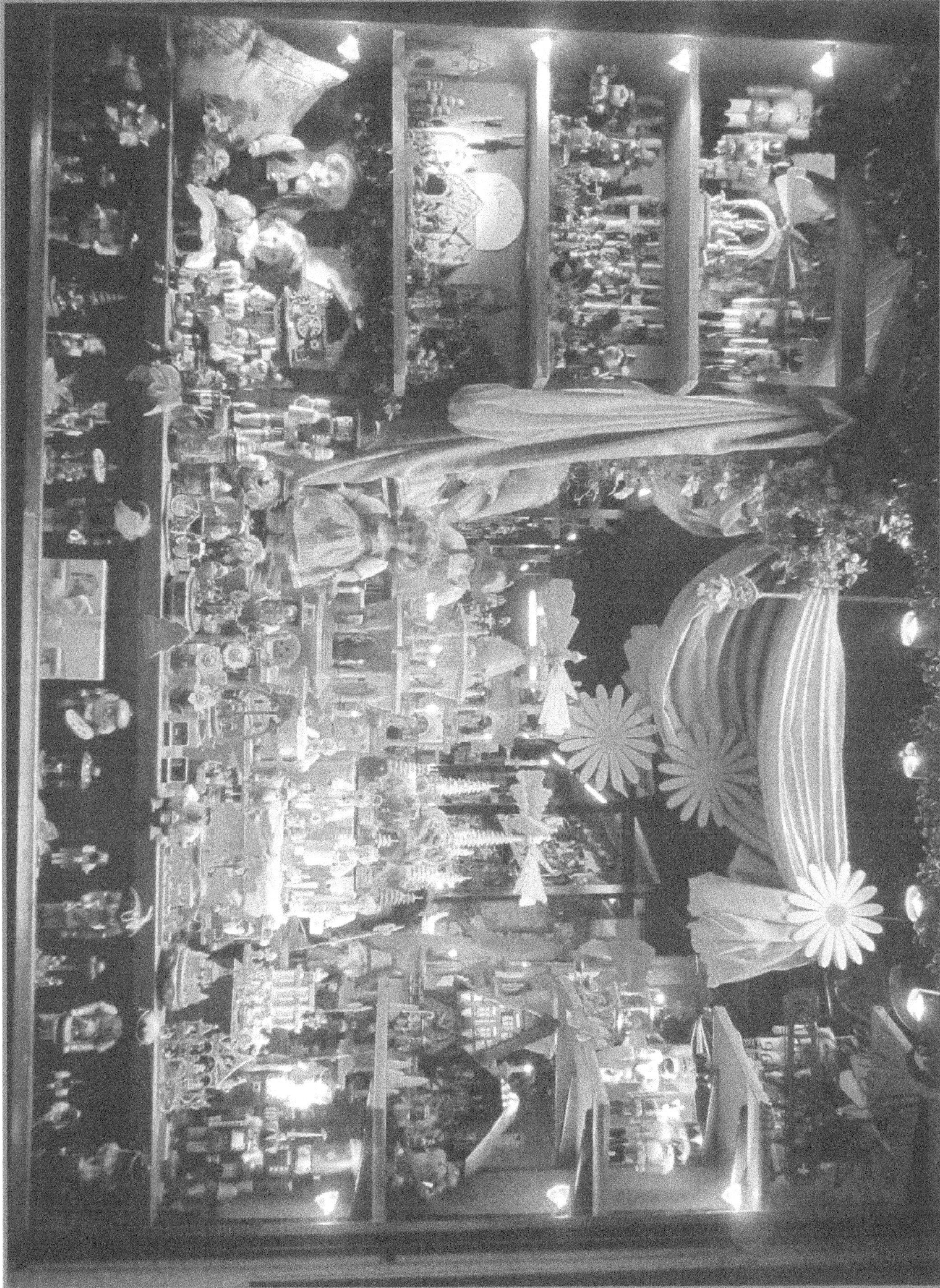

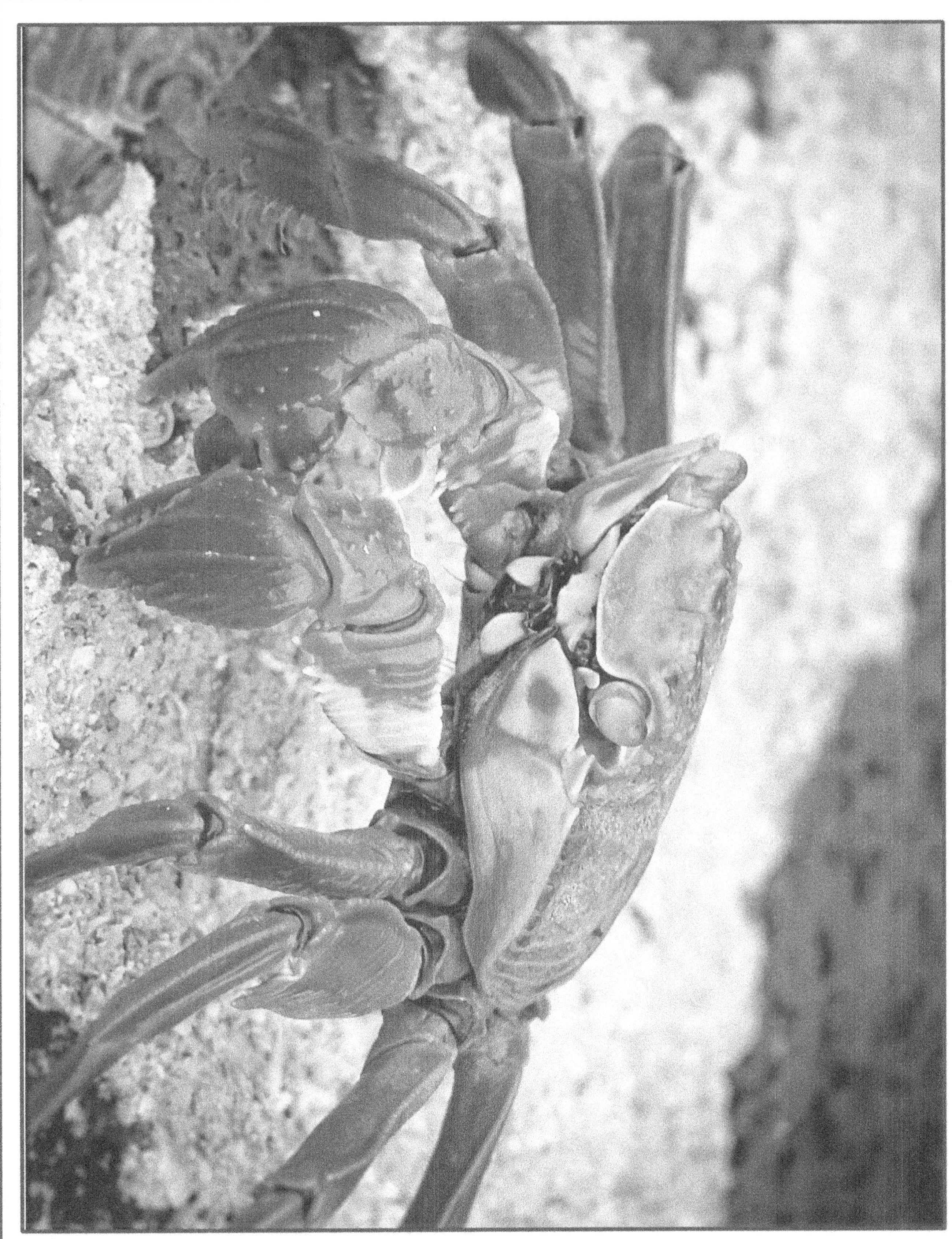

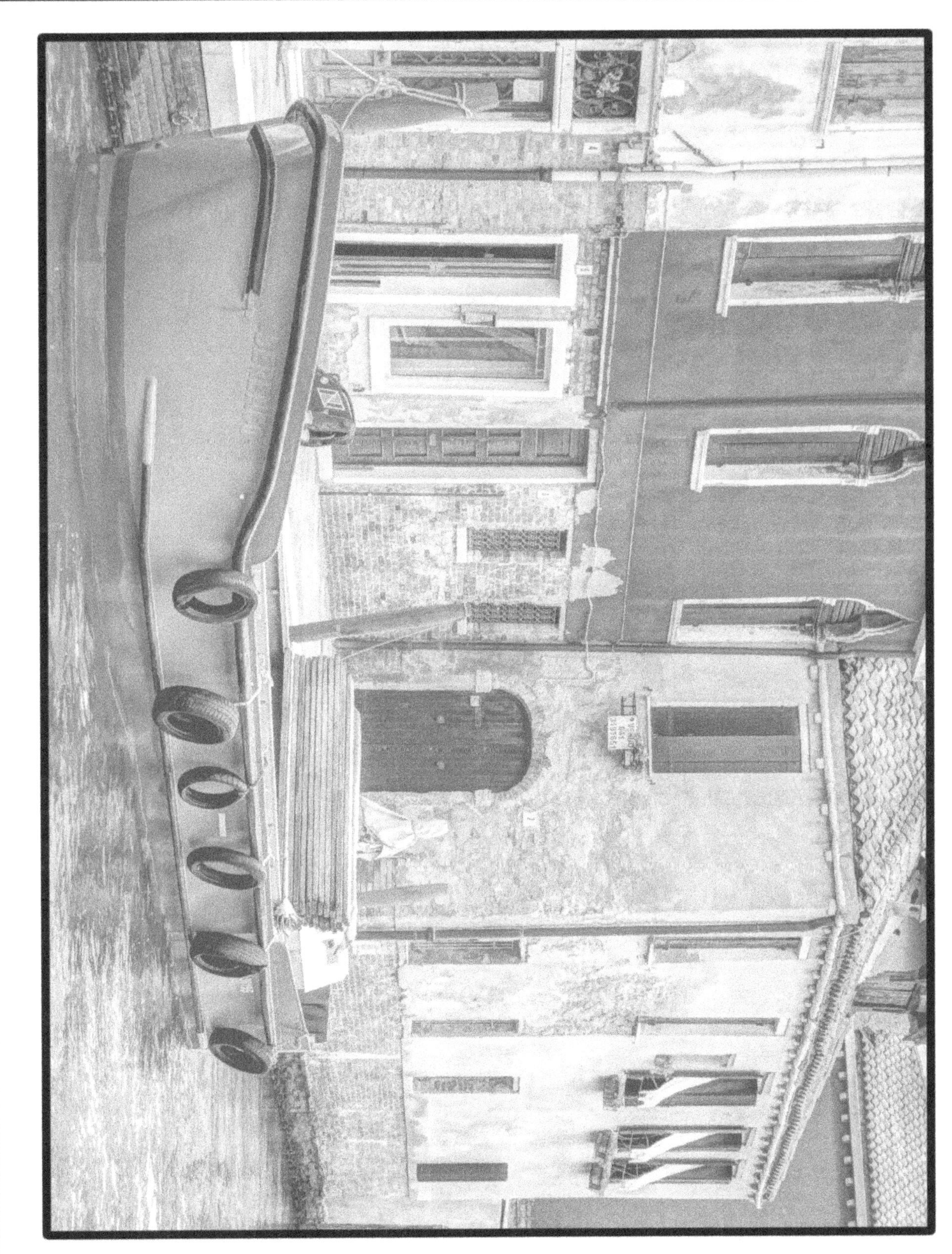

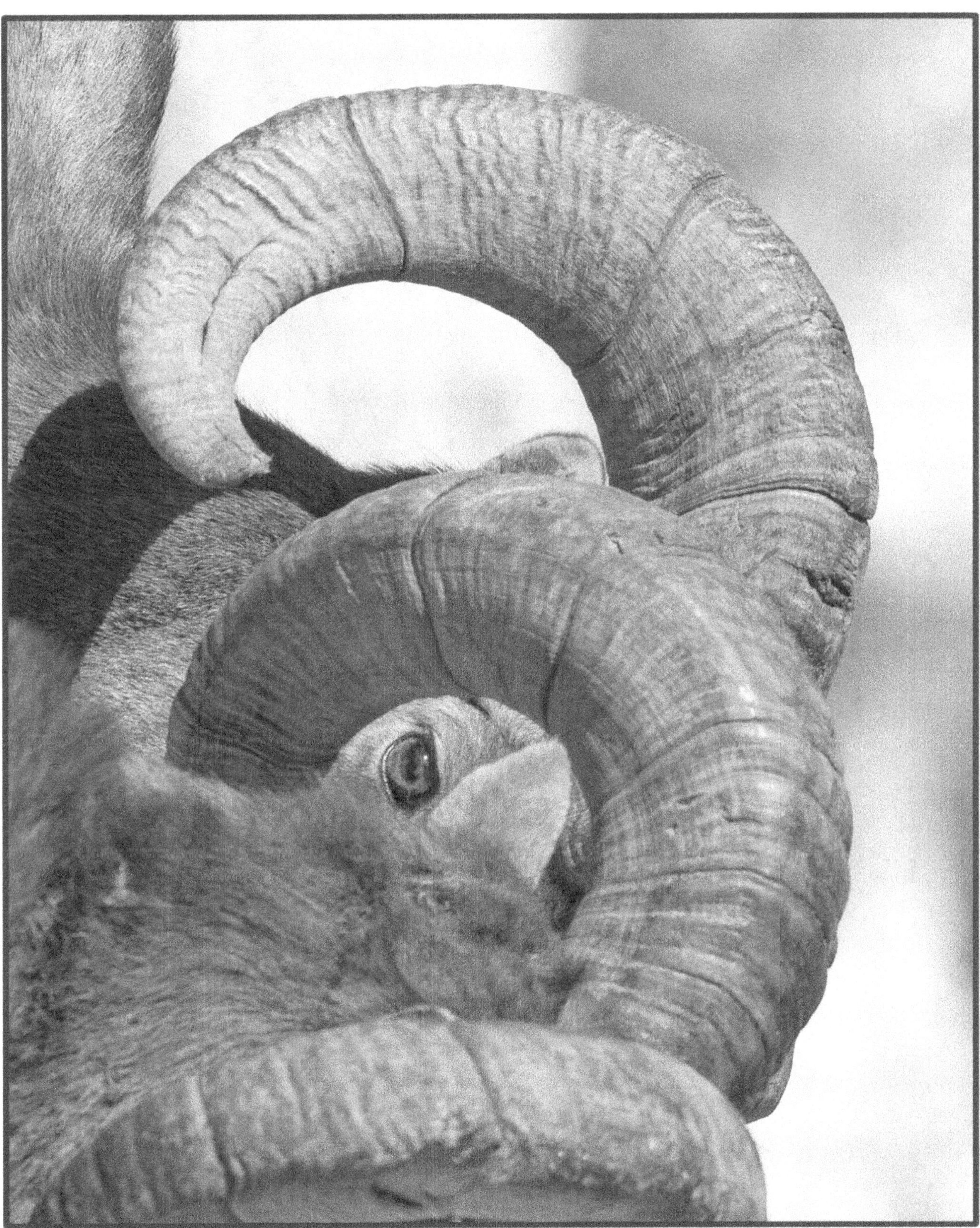

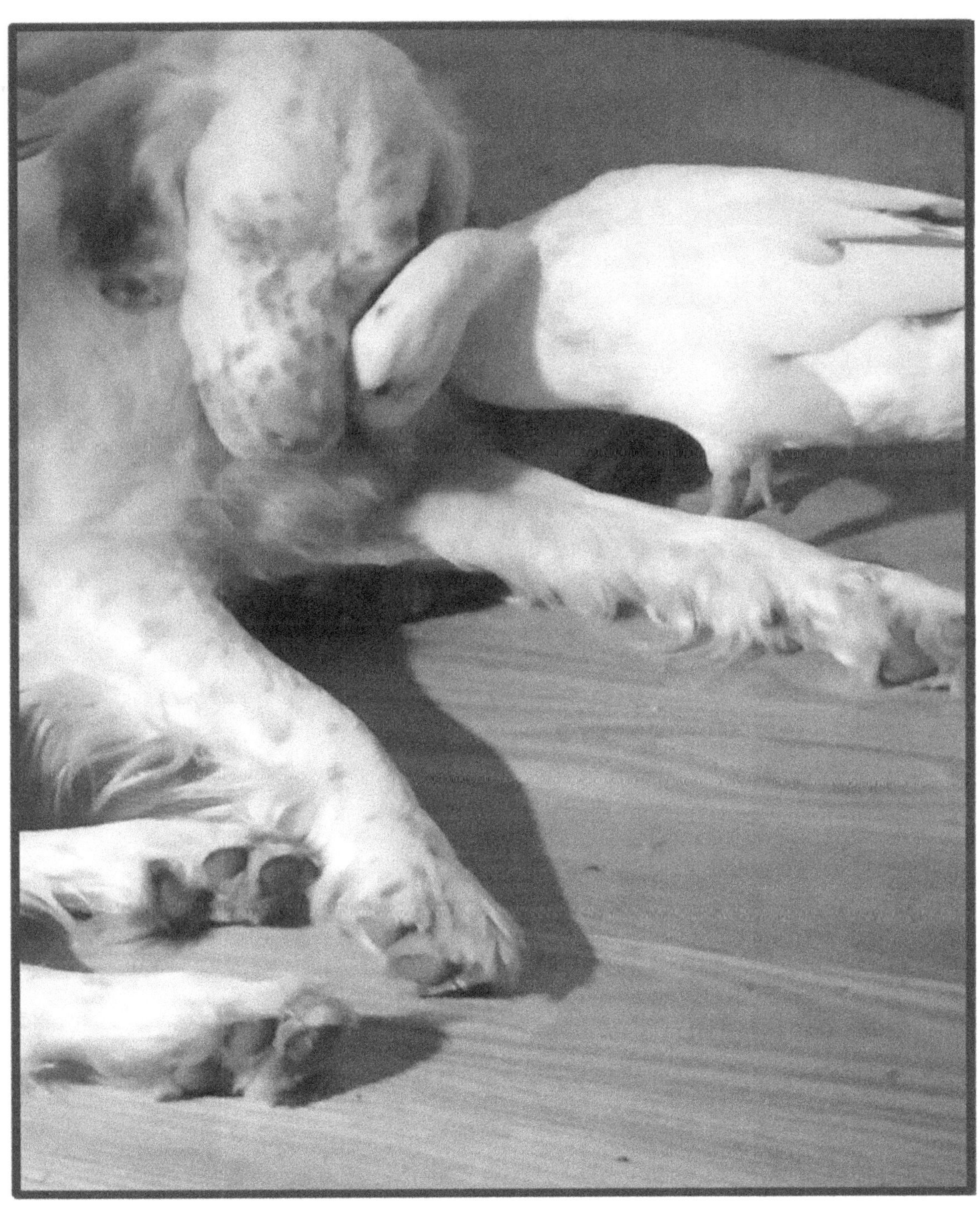

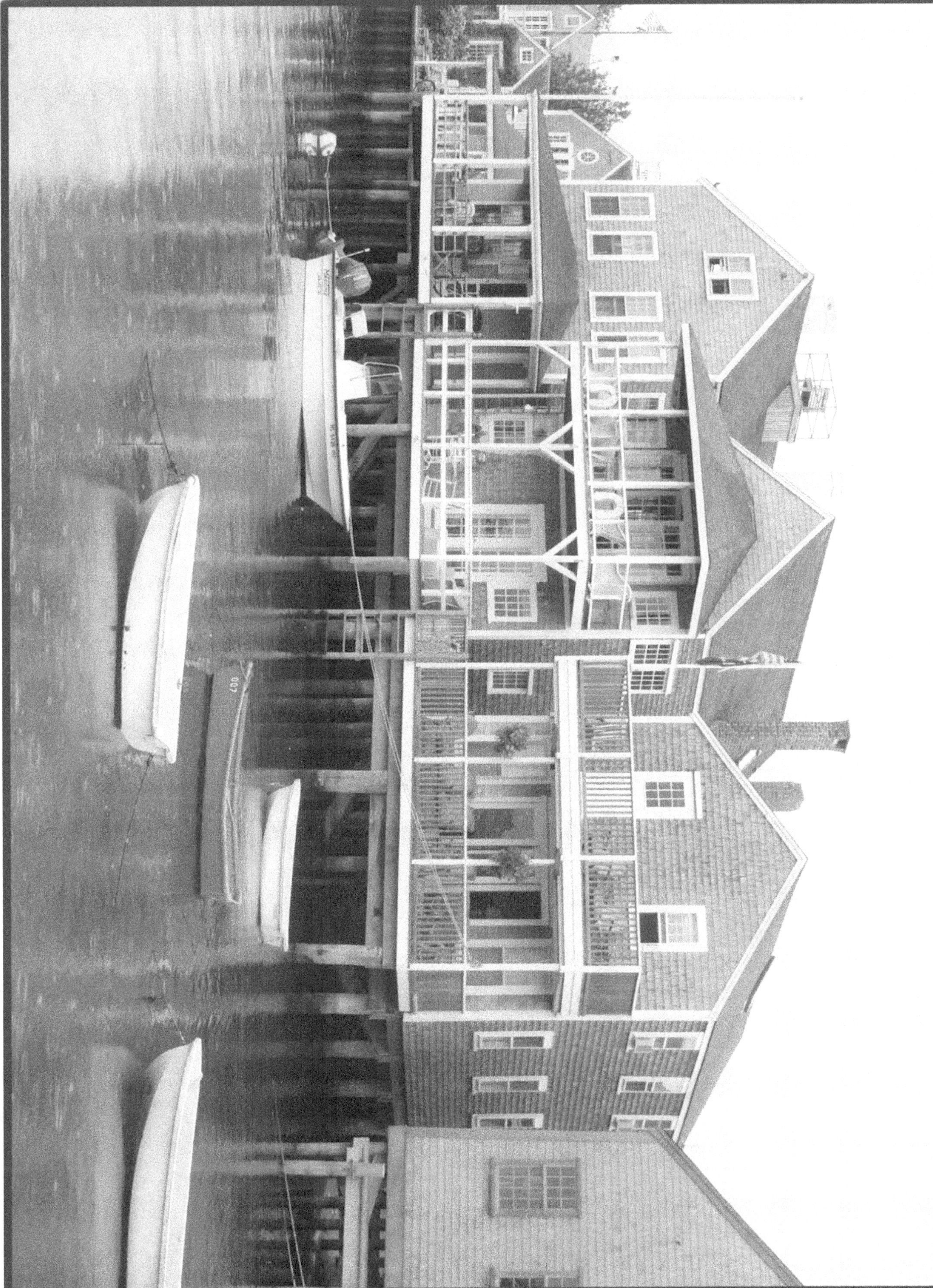

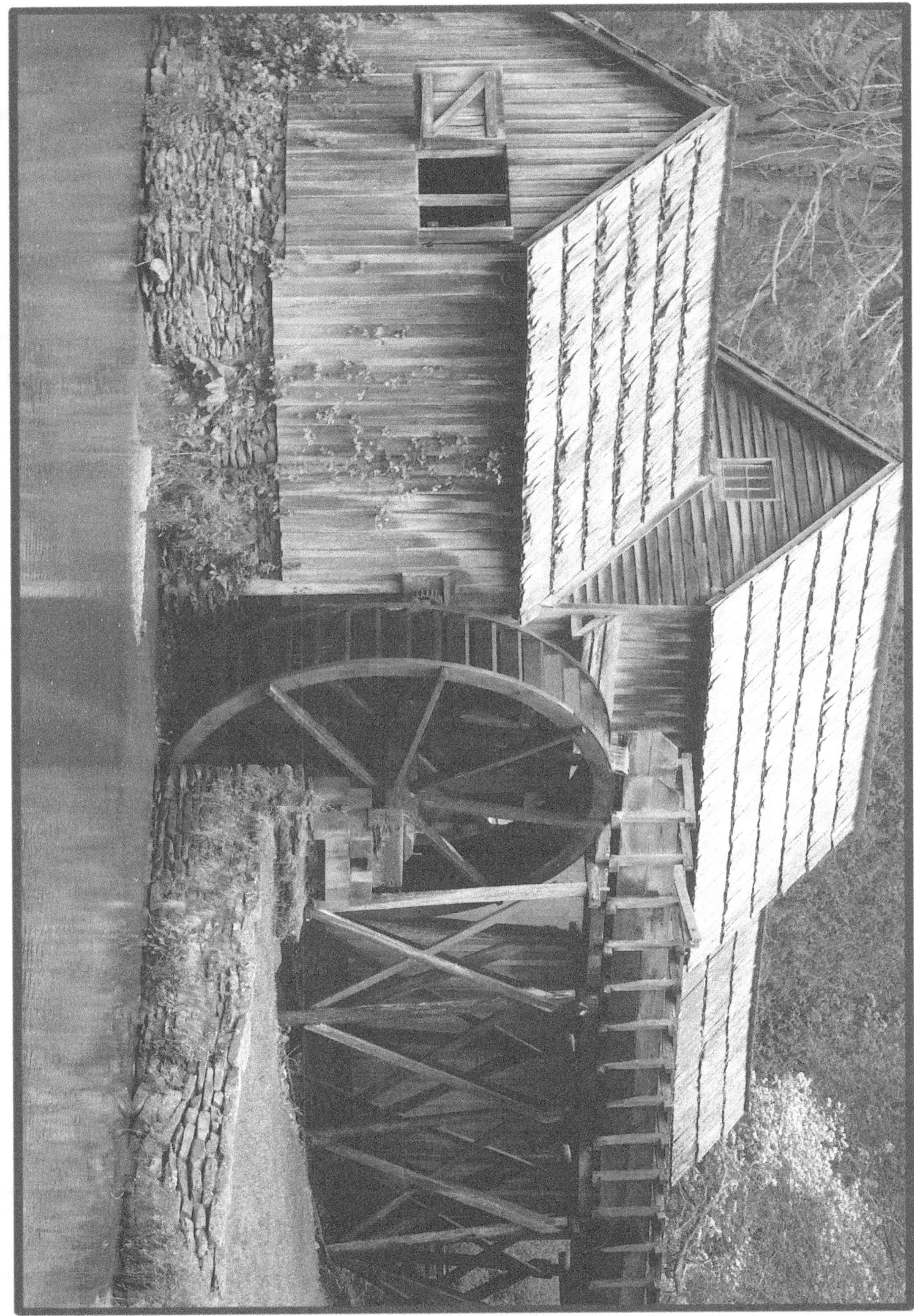

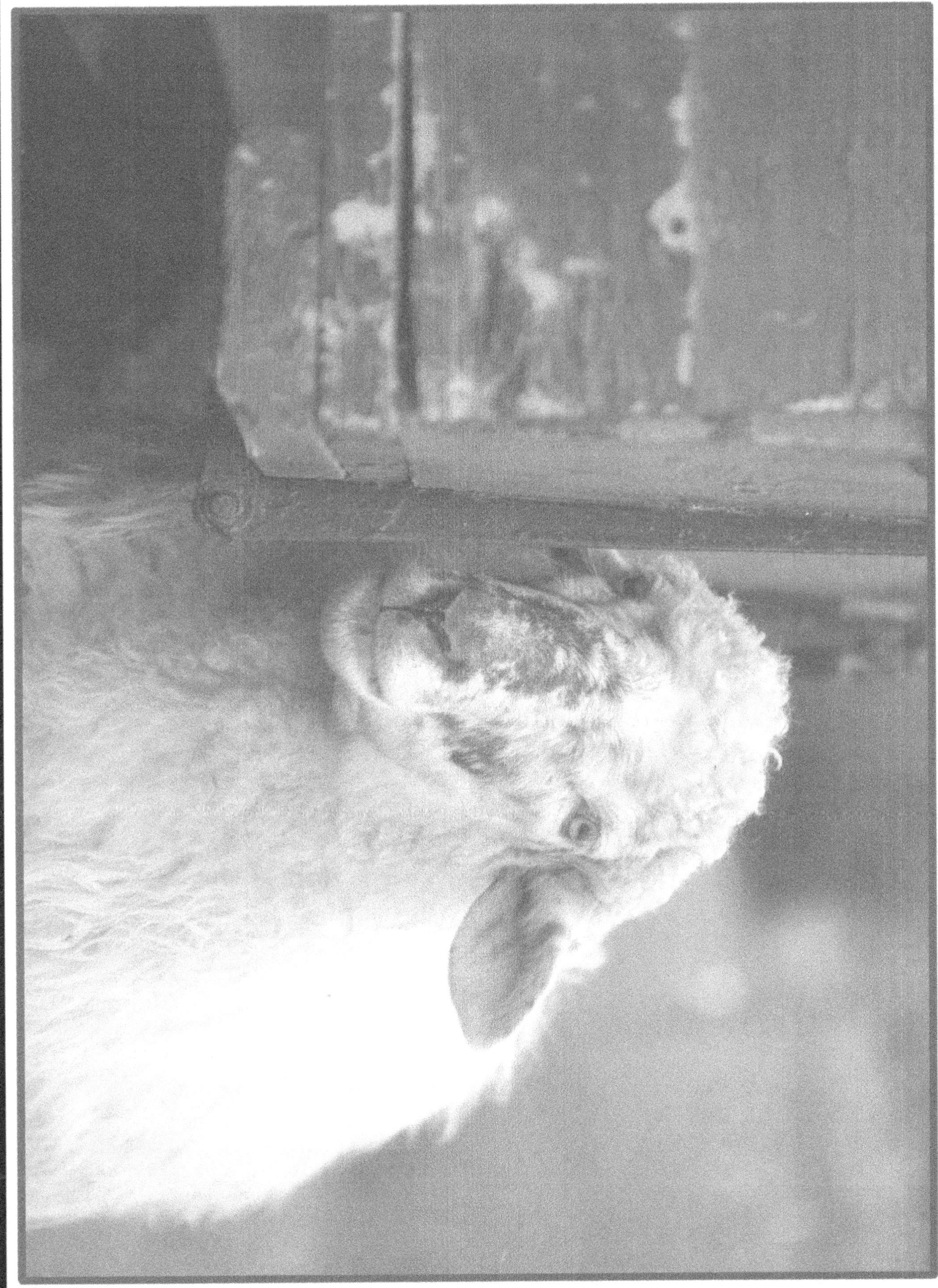

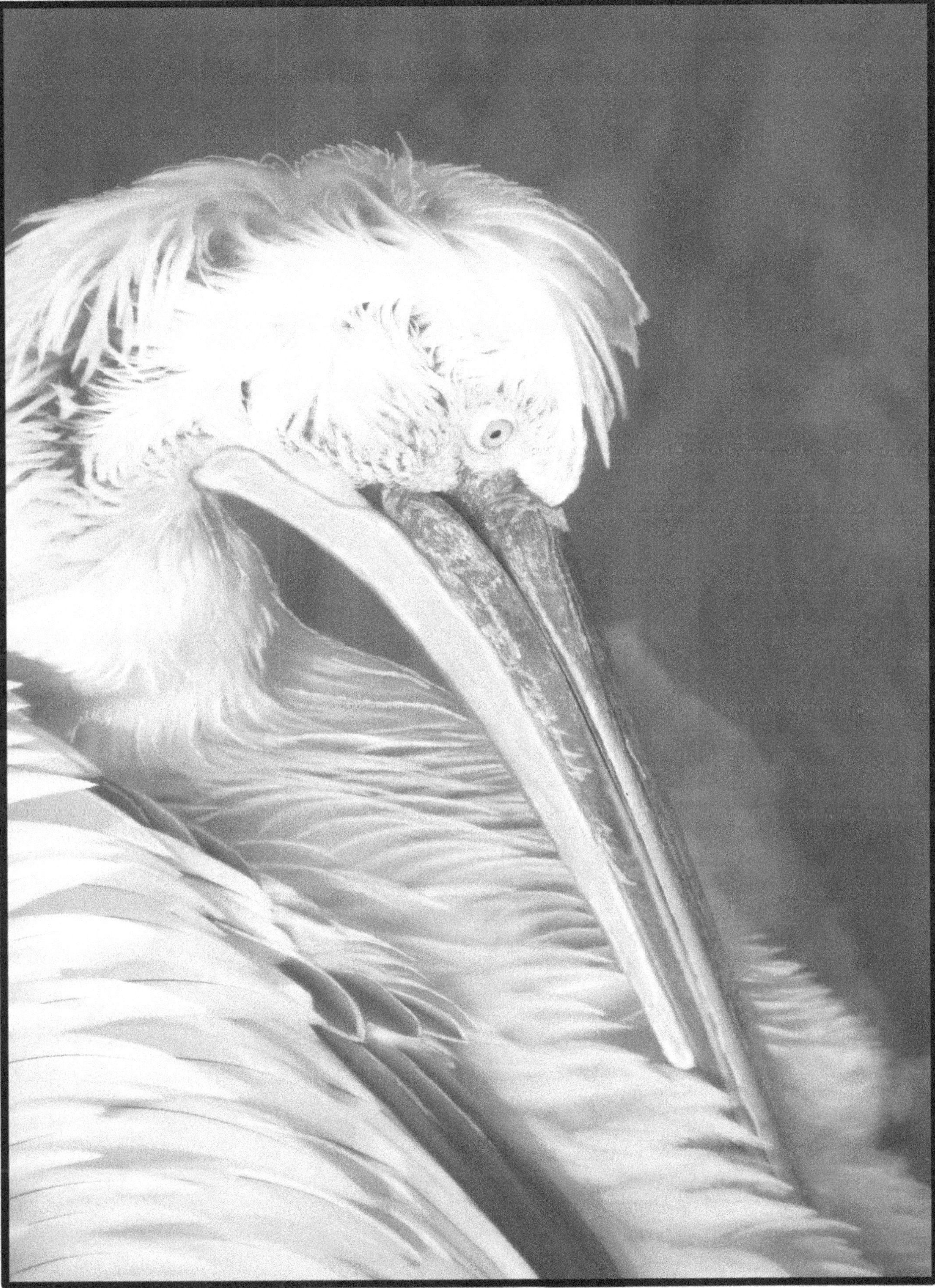

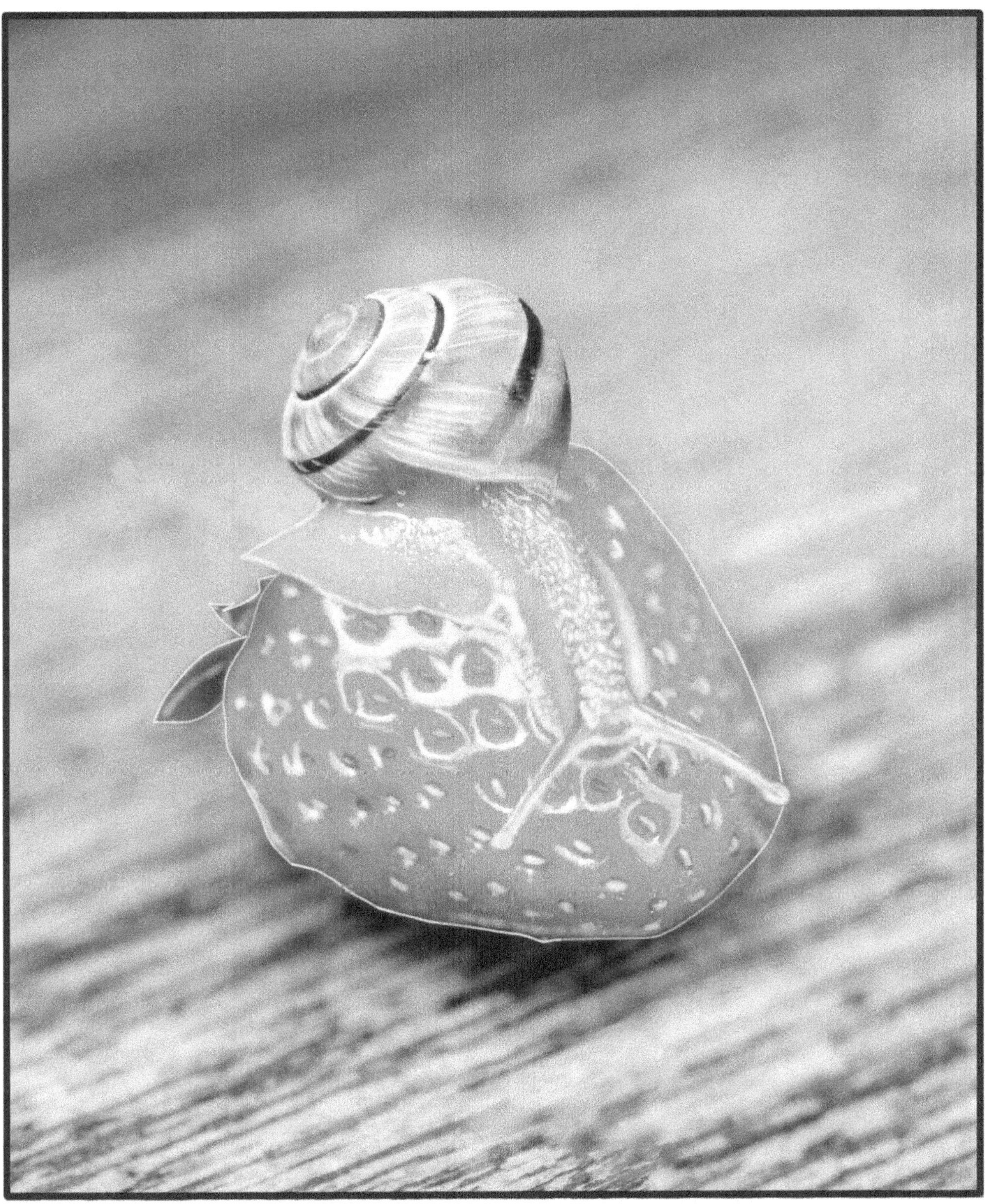

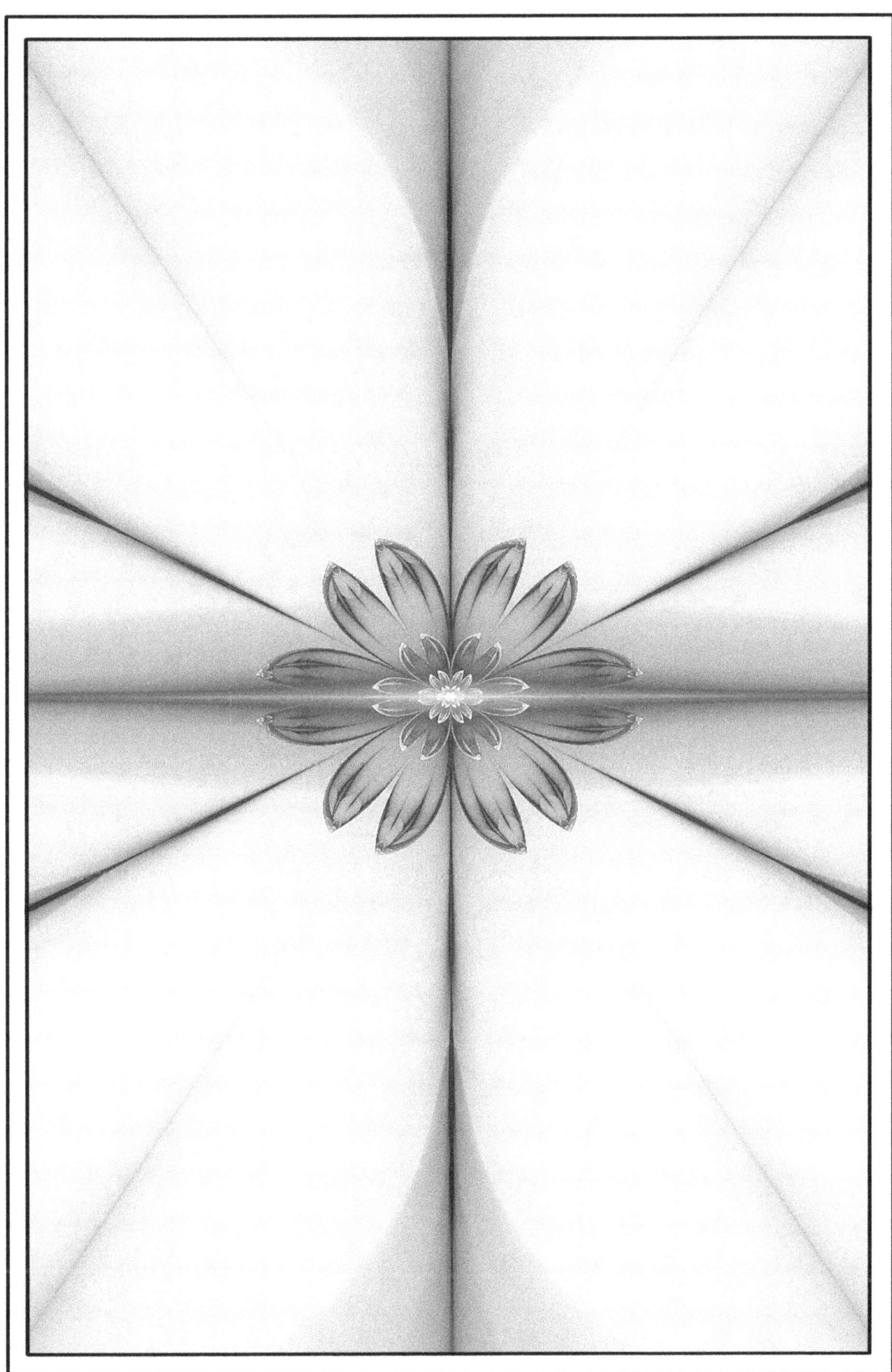

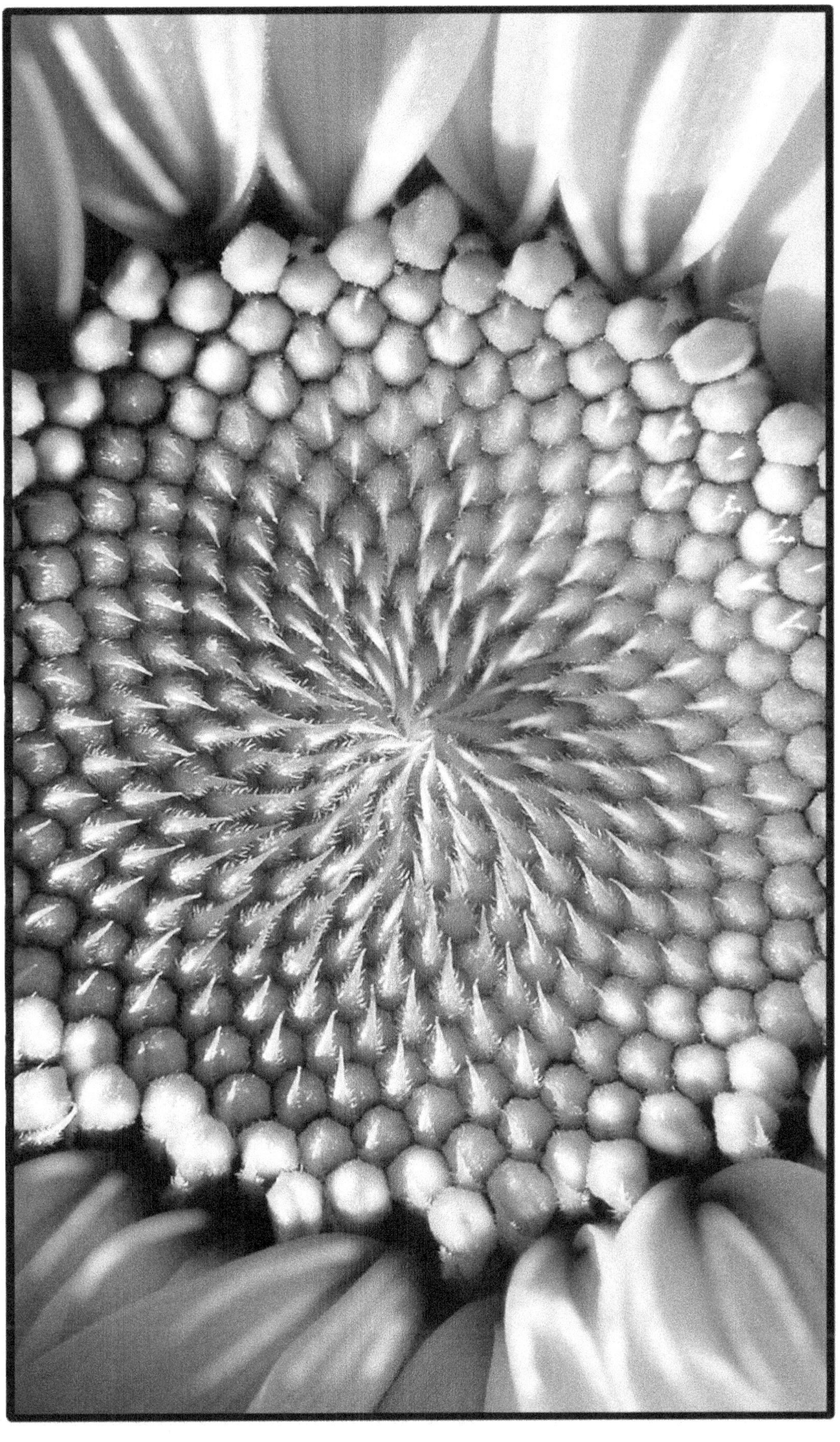

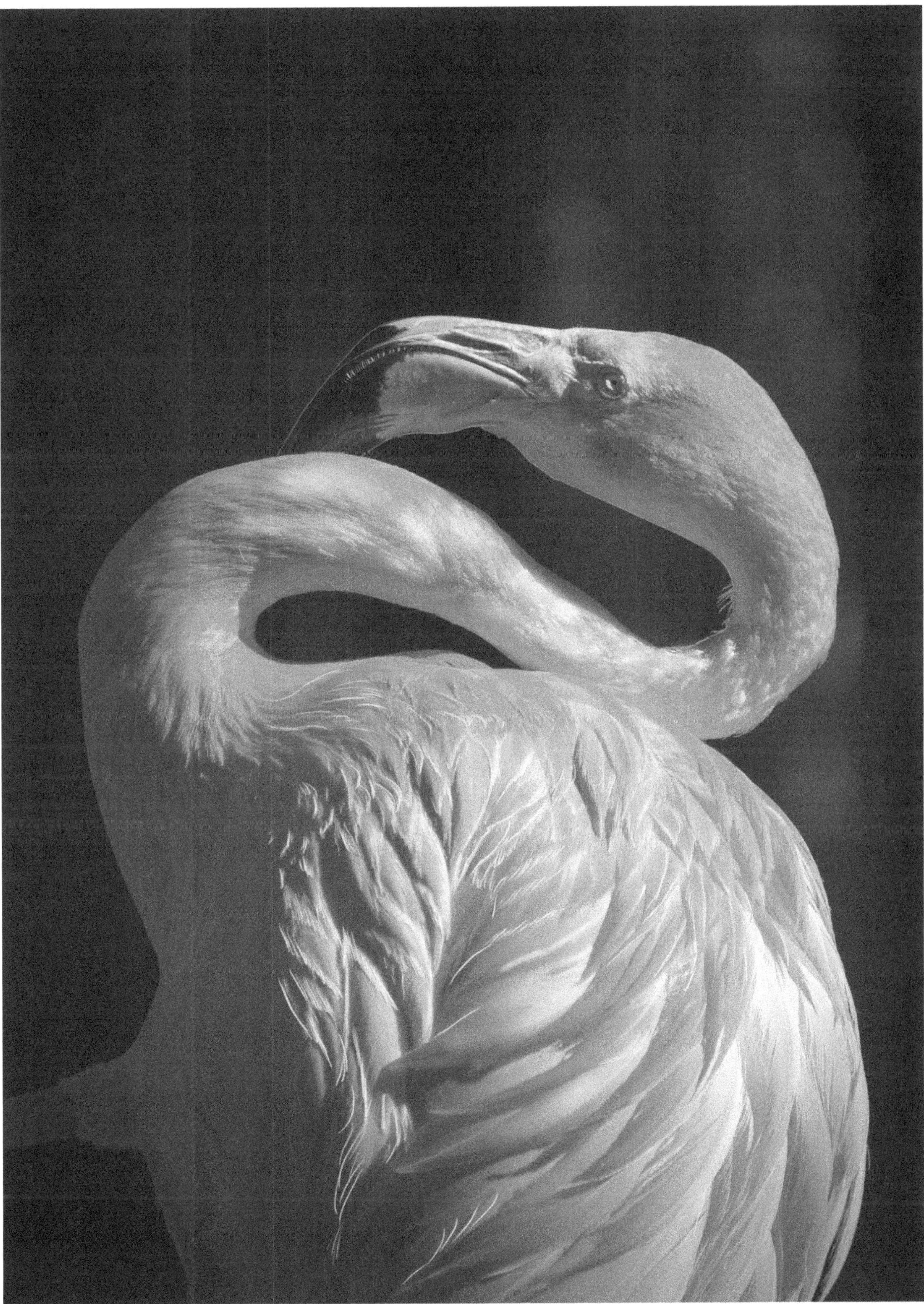

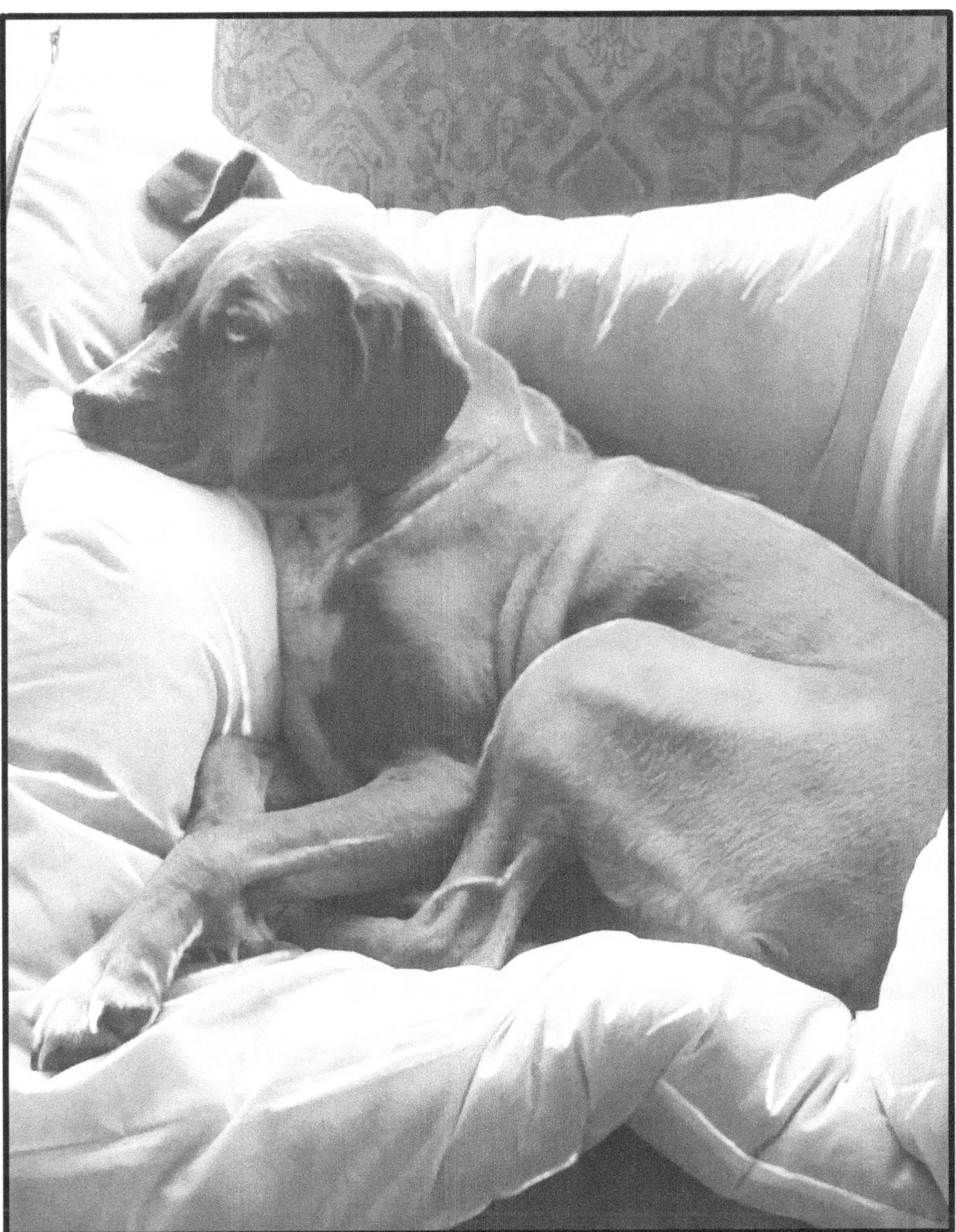

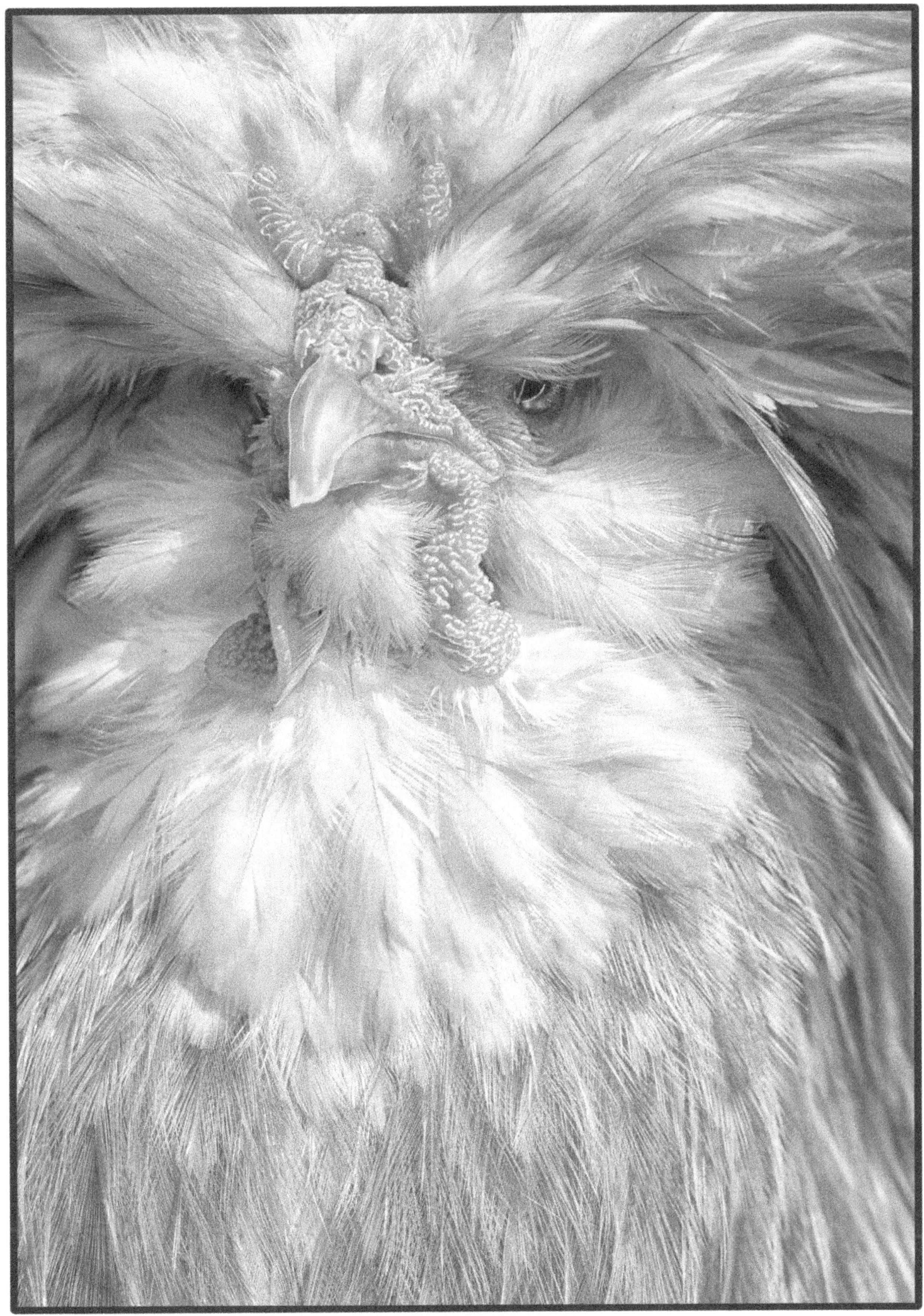

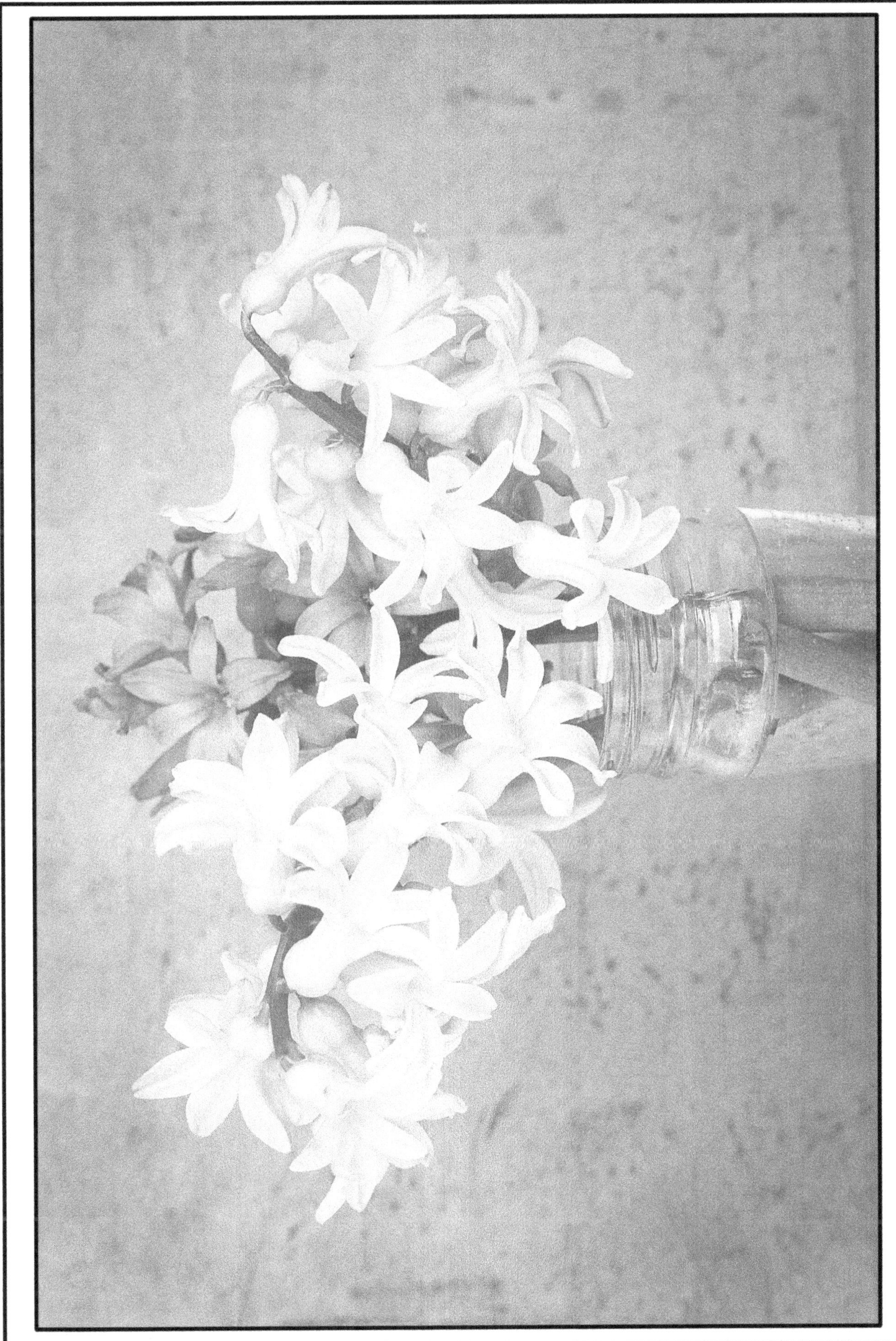

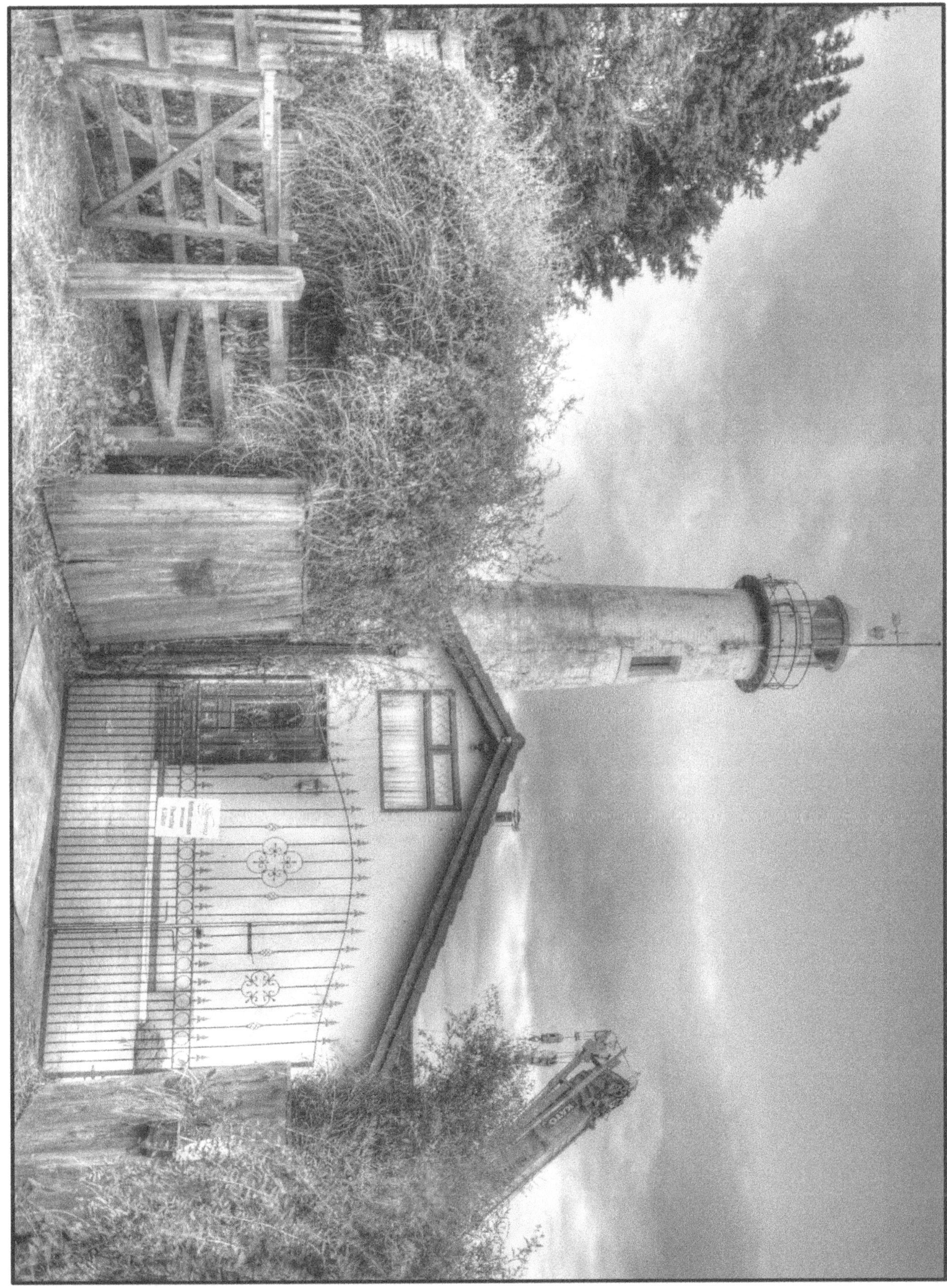

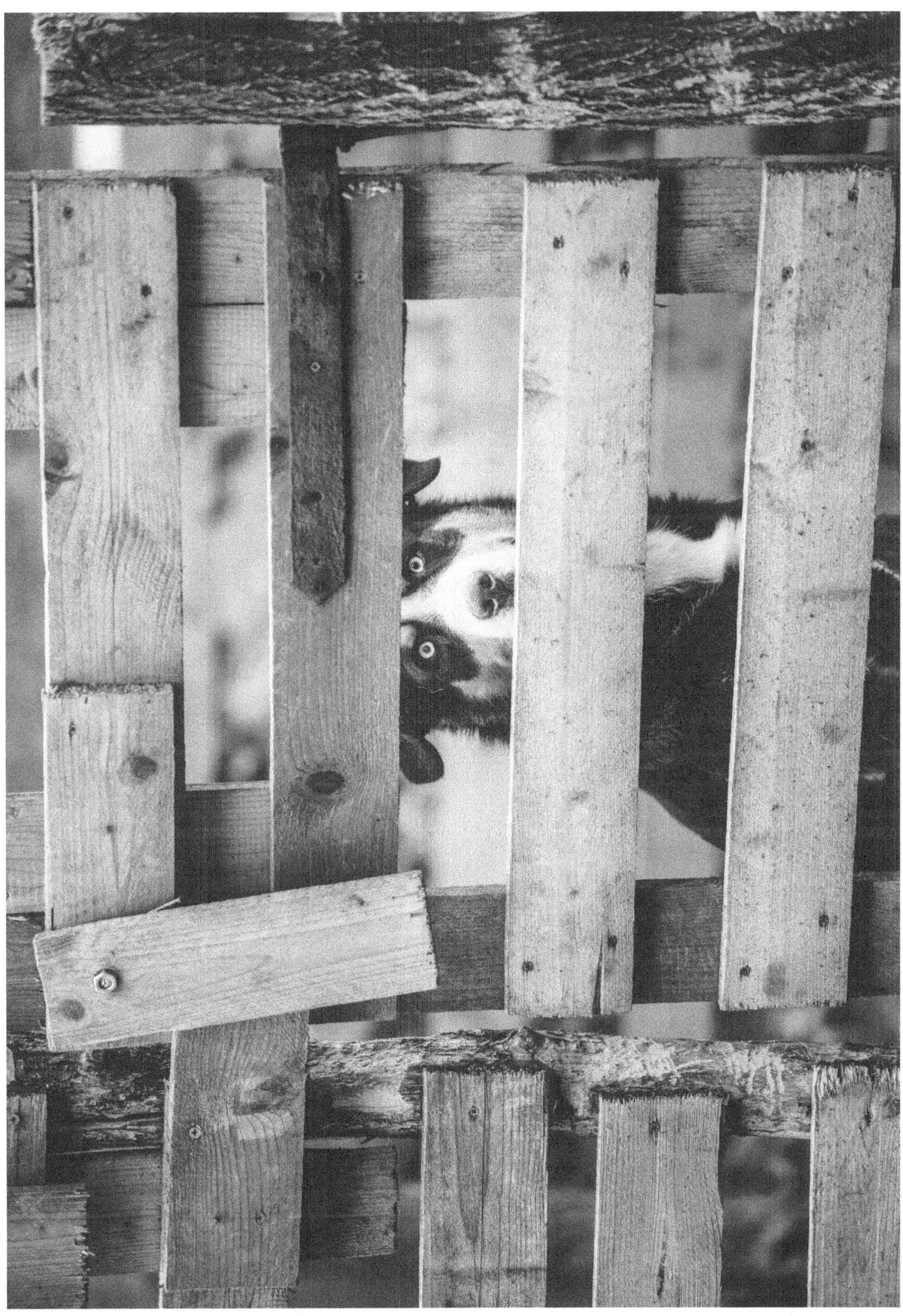